third edition

COMMUNICATION STUDIES
Fundamentals of Speech Communication
Student Handbook
103

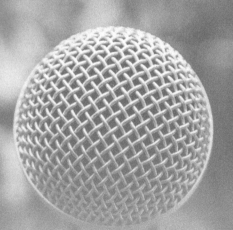

Kendall Hunt
publishing company

Cover image © Shutterstock, Inc.

Kendall Hunt
publishing company

www.kendallhunt.com
Send all inquiries to:
4050 Westmark Drive
Dubuque, IA 52004-1840

Table of Contents

Dear Student,

Welcome to Fundamentals of Speech Communication. Whether this is your first semester or very last, we are happy you have decided to join us. Public speaking is frequently listed as one of Americans' top fears in public opinion polls. Comedian Jerry Seinfeld once joked that at a funeral, people would rather be in the casket than giving the eulogy! You may feel like one of those people today. Conversely, you may be happy and excited to be in this class. Either way, we promise to do our best to help you become the best speaker you can be by the end of the semester.

How are we going to do that? This course is designed to enhance the development of critical thinking skills and their application to verbal and non-verbal interaction in interpersonal and public communication contexts. What that means is that you are going to learn about communication. You will leave this class understanding the importance of communication in public settings and with some experience communicating about public issues. We also hope this course helps foster a sense of civic engagement in students.

Civic engagement can mean a lot of different things. It's everything from volunteering in your local community to getting involved with international issues. It's working with other people, at any level, to try to solve a problem and make things better. It can be as small as you deciding to pick up litter at the park. It can be as large as joining Peace Corps. Lots of people tend to think of only political things like voting when they hear civic engagement, but we are more interested in talking with you about problem-solving, meaning how people come together to solve problems they can't fix on their own.

Ultimately, we want classes like CMM 103 to make you feel more comfortable to speak out on behalf of a problem that you care about. We want to help you find your voice and learn how to use it. We want you to see that you shouldn't be afraid of standing before your peers and sharing information and concerns with them. By the end of the semester, we hope you leave this class feeling a little more empowered to communicate about the things that matter to you.

This workbook is designed to supplement the class by providing hard copies of worksheets, guidelines, and rubrics you will need in this course. Please bring it with you to each class session. We will look forward to working with you this semester and developing your voice as a citizen. You may have 99 problems, but public speaking will not be one by the end of the semester!

Marshall University

Course Title/ Number/Section	**Fundamentals of Speech Communication/CMM 103 SECTION:**
Semester/Year	
Days/Time	
Location	
Professor	
Office	
Phone	
Email	
Office Hours	
Basic Course Director Contact Information	Dr. Jill C. Underhill Smith Hall 250 underhillj@marshall.edu
University Policies	By enrolling in this course, you agree to the University Policies listed below. Please read the full text of each policy be going to www.marshall.edu/academic-affairs and clicking on "Marshall University Policies." Or, you can access the policies directly by going to http://www.marshall.edu/academic-affairs/?page_id=802 Academic Dishonesty/ Excused Absence Policy for Undergraduates/ Computing Services Acceptable Use/ Inclement Weather/ Dead Week/ Students with Disabilities/ Academic Forgiveness/ Academic Probation and Suspension/ Academic Rights and Responsibilities of Students/ Affirmative Action/ Sexual Harassment

Required Materials

Underhill, J. C. (2017). Fundaments of Speech Communication Workbook. Kendall Hunt Publishing. ISBN: 9781524937195

The workbook is available in the Marshall University bookstore.

Coopman, S. J. & Lull, J. (2017). *Public Speaking: The Evolving Art* (4th Edition). Stamford, CT: Wadsworth Publisher.

Book ISBN: 978-1-337-10756-3

Loose-leaf Edition ISBN: 978-1-337-10984-0

The textbook is available for rent or purchase in the bookstore. You also can rent or purchase the book online. Please make sure you order for the FOURTH EDITION. You do not need to order Mindtap or any additional Cengage products.

Course Description

A course designed to enhance the development of critical thinking skills and their application to verbal and nonverbal interaction in interpersonal and public communication contexts.

Course Philosophy

CMM 103 is a part of the university's general education requirements. We believe that communication is a fundamental and essential part of life. We also believe that improving both your understanding of communication and the ability to communicate effectively will serve you well in your career, your relationships, and your civic life. This course is designed to help you become more confident, more articulate, and better able to interpret the communication of others.

Relationships among Course, Program, and Degree Profile Outcomes

Course Outcomes	How Accomplished in this Course	How Evaluated in this Course

Students will be able to recognize communication as a transactional process by

Determining audience orientation toward the topic	Classroom activities Audience Evaluation Survey Peer Evaluations	Speech Proposals Oral Presentations Critical Listening Exam
Identifying supporting material most relevant to the audience	Lecture Activities Peer Evaluations	Speech Proposals Supporting a Claim Creating an Argument Oral Presentations Preparation Outlines Critical Listening Exam
Recognizing and adjusting to nonverbal audience feedback	Lecture Activities Peer Evaluations	Oral Presentations Critical Listening Exams

Students will learn to demonstrate critical thinking in the production and evaluation of communication events by

Differentiating between various types of evidence	Lecture Classroom Activities	Speech Proposals Oral Presentations Preparation Outlines Exam
Extrapolating valid claims from evidence	Lecture Classroom Activities	Creating an Argument Persuasive Speech Preparation Outlines Self Evaluation Critical Listening Exam
Identifying and producing fact, value, and policy claims	Lecture Classroom Activities	Creating an Argument Speech Proposals Persuasive Speech Preparation Outlines Critical Listening Exam
Identifying the types of reasoning that link evidence to claims	Lecture Classroom Activities	Creating an Argument Persuasive Speech Preparation Outlines Critical Listening Self Evaluation Exam
Identifying the limitations of evidence	Lecture Classroom Activities	Creating an Argument Persuasive Speech Critical Listening Exam
Identifying weaknesses in argument and reasoning	Lecture Classroom Activities Peer Evaluations	Creating an Argument Speech Proposals Persuasive Speech Critical Listening Self Evaluation Exam
Producing valid arguments	Lecture Classroom Activities Peer Evaluations	Creating an Argument Persuasive Speech Critical Listening Self Evaluation Exam

Students will produce organized informative and persuasive presentations by

Demonstrating the ability to capture the audience attention	Lecture Classroom Activities Peer Evaluations	Oral Presentations Preparation Outlines Speech Proposals Self Evaluation Critical Listening Exam
Stating the thesis and previewing their oral remarks	Lecture Classroom Activities Peer Evaluations	Oral Presentations Preparation Outlines Self Evaluation Critical Listening Exam
Using transitions and signposts to emphasize speech structure	Lecture Classroom Activities Peer Evaluations	Oral Presentations Preparation Outlines Self Evaluation Critical Listening Exam
Concluding their remarks with a summary of the main points	Lecture Classroom Activities Peer Evaluations	Oral Presentations Preparation Outlines Self Evaluation Critical Listening Exam

Students will develop effective extemporaneous speaking skills by

Maintaining eye contact with the audience while speaking	Lecture Classroom Activities Peer Evaluations	Oral Presentation Self Evaluation Critical Listening Exam
Using gestures that complement the verbal message	Lecture Classroom Activities Peer Evaluations	Oral Presentation Self Evaluation Critical Listening Exam
Speaking with varied vocal cues	Lecture Classroom Activities Peer Evaluations	Oral Presentation Self Evaluation Critical Listening Exam

Attendance

Attendance will be taken at each session. You are allowed _____ personal days during the semester (on days that do not include your oral presentations). These absences do not include illnesses that require medical care or university-sponsored events. You do not need to contact your instructor to tell him/her that you are using the unexcused absence.

After hitting the limit on unexcused absences, you will lose 10 points from your total grade for each additional absence.

Also, you need to attend the class on time. It is your responsibility to make sure that you are counted as attending if you come to the class after attendance is taken. See your instructor after the class to change your attendance status. **Being late to the class twice is equivalent to one unexcused absence.**

You must attend the sessions you are scheduled to present a speech. If you miss an oral presentation, you must have an excused absence to reschedule without penalty. If you miss your presentation day and do not have an excused absence, you will automatically be penalized one letter grade off your total score. You are expected to be ready to present on return, and will be further penalized another letter grade for each session missed after your scheduled presentation date. Excused absences must be documented to the Dean of Students. Please feel free to check with your instructor about attendance at any point during the semester.

Assignment Policies

You must present every assigned speech and presentation in front of a live audience to pass the class. Failure to present any of the assigned speeches in front of an audience will result in failing the course, regardless of the total points earned.

Unless explicitly stated, written assignments will be submitted electronically via the drop box function on the Blackboard. If you have trouble submitting via the Blackboard, email the assignment to the instructor before the deadline for a full credit.

All assignments should be **typed in 12-point font, double-spaced, with one inch margins on all sides**.

Please proofread your work! Typos and grammatical errors may result in a lower grade on the assignment.

Late assignments will not be accepted for full credit unless the instructor has given prior consent. For every 24 hours that the assignment is late without the instructor's approval, the assignment grade will drop by 20%. The assignment will not be accepted later than five business days after it is due.

Recording Policy

Each of your speeches will be recorded and uploaded to the Blackboard for an easy online access. Although many of us find seeing ourselves on video a disconcerting experience, it is an excellent way of improving your public speaking performances. We have an annual assessment program for our course, and your speech may be submitted to that assessment. If you object to your speech being submitted for confidential assessment, please let me know.

Questions about grades

All questions about graded assignments or exams must be brought to the instructor within one week from the day the grade is posted. Your instructor will schedule an appointment to discuss the assignment outside of class time.

Consultations

Please do not wait until the night an assignment is due to realize that you are unsure of what is expected. Uncertainties can always exist. It is your instructor's intention to do everything she/he can to help you learn the material of the course. If you do not understand an assignment, ask. The excuse, "I didn't know what was expected," will not be accepted as a justification for poor performance.

Email Policy

Email is the preferred medium for contacting your instructor. It should be used to set up appointments and ask short questions. The instructor will generally respond to your inquiry in one business day.

Classroom Policies

Let us make our classroom an oasis of civility. Please do not use your cell phone during class hours. The use of cell phones in class is acceptable only in case of an emergency that requires you to dial 911 or the campus police. **The first time you use your cell phone in class, I will ask you to put it away. Thereafter, I may ask you to leave the class for the day and count it against your attendance record.**

Students arriving late are not to disrupt presentations, but should remain quietly outside the classroom until the speaker is finished. Anyone needing to leave early should inform me before the class, sit near the door, and leave in between presentations.

Academic Dishonesty

Plagiarism: Copying another's work without proper citation of the source constitutes plagiarism. Using a speech that someone else wrote is also plagiarism. Plagiarism in any form will not be tolerated. A student found plagiarizing another's work will automatically receive an "F" on the assignment and may be subject to further university discipline.

This policy includes "sharing" speeches across sections and semesters. We use Safe Assign and sample a large number of speech videos each semester to view for assessment. **If it is discovered that two students have given exactly the same speech, they will both be reported to the Dean of Students, and further university discipline with the recommendation of suspension or expulsion from the university will be recommended.**

Cheating

According to the university policy, cheating is defined as the use of any unauthorized materials during an academic exercise that the use of which is prohibited. Cheating also includes viewing of another person's work or securing any part of an assignment or examination in advance of the distribution by the instructor. For this class, you are allowed to use all the notes and course material when taking the reading quizzes. You are asked, however, to take the quizzes on your own and not copy anyone else's work. Cheating will not be tolerated in this class, and will result automatically in an "F" for your total quiz grade in the course.

Course Requirements

Coursework and Quizzes

Reading Quizzes (16 chapters × 5 points each)	80
In-Class Activities/Participation Points	75
Reflections -Informative speech (15 points) -Persuasive speech (15 points)	30
Total	185

Strategic Planning Assignments

Informative speech proposal	50
Informative speech preparation outline	50
Persuasive speech proposal	50
Persuasive speech preparation outline	75
Informative peer review	20
Persuasive peer review	20
Total	265

Oral Assignments
(Speeches should be presented to an audience to pass the course)

Informative Speech	100
Persuasive Speech	150
Ceremonial Speech	50
Total	300

Grading   **TOTAL POINTS FOR THE COURSE**   **750**

A (100–90%)	750 – 675
B (89–80%)	674 – 600
C (79–70%)	599 – 525
D (69–60%)	524 – 450
F (59–0%)	Less than 450 points

Student Data Sheet

Section:

Student Name:

Current Class Standing:

Major: Minor:

Professional Aspirations:

Current Employment, Clubs, Organizations, and/or other commitments:

Past experience in communication classes or communication-related activities:

Is there any personal information you'd like me to know about you? (illness, communication anxiety, etc.?)

What are the learning goals you have for this class? Is there a topic or idea that you hope we will discuss during the semester?

Characteristics of Critical Thinking

Define what each characteristic of critical thinking means in your own words.

1. Critical thinkers are reluctant to accept assertions on faith.

2. Critical thinkers distinguish facts from opinions.

3. Critical thinkers seek to uncover assumptions.

4. Critical thinkers are open to new ideas.

5. Critical thinkers apply reason and common sense to new ideas.

6. Critical thinkers relate new ideas to what they already know.

Listening for Logical Fallacies

Logical fallacies are flaws in reasoning. Through careful listening, critical thinkers are able to identify and reject logical fallacies. Some of the most common logical fallacies used by past CMM 103 students are listed below.

For more logical fallacies, visit: http://yourlogicalfallacyis.com

Most Common

Hasty Generalizations—a speaker cites an example as evidence for widespread occurrence.

Slippery Slope—the claim that some sort of chain reaction will happen, usually resulting in some terrible consequence.

Testimonials—a well-known figure provides an endorsement for a product. Sometimes this person's notoriety has little to do with the product they endorse.

Ad Populum/Band Wagon—the idea that you should be swayed by popular opinion alone.

Rewards—the claim that you will receive personal benefits for purchasing a product or agreeing with the speaker.

Ad hominem (attacking the person)—arguing against an issue by personally attacking the opposition.

Exercise

Identify the type of logical fallacy below.

1. "The majority of West Virginia residents do not support the legalization of marijuana. Therefore, we should not legalize marijuana."

2. "Kentucky Senator Rand Paul has expressed support for states deciding to legalize medicinal marijuana. He was a dope-smoker in college, so his opinion does not matter."

3.	Miley Cyrus used to be a wholesome girl on family television. Then, she started smoking marijuana every day. Now, she twerks on anything that moves and dyes her body hair pink. Think about your little sister or cousins. Every day, little girls are starting to smoke pot and twerk. Let's stop marijuana legalization and save these little girls.

4.	Bruce Springsteen, known as the Boss to our parents, is considered one of the most creative musicians of the 20th century. He stated in an interview for the book "Bruce Springsteen: Two Hearts: The definitive biography 1972-2003" that he never did any kind of drug. He just wanted to focus on his music. He also stated that he does not believe there are any positive benefits for doing drugs. If a talented musician is against using marijuana, you should be too.

5.	If we legalize medicinal marijuana, too many people will exploit the system with fake symptoms to get their hands on it. Suddenly everyone will have a medical problem that requires marijuana, and doctors looking to make money will hand out scripts without blinking their eyes. We are going to have a large part of our population high as kites 24/7. There are going to be more car accidents, crimes, and broken families. Junkies unable to get their next fix will kill for it. If we legalize any type of marijuana in this state, lots of people will die.

6.	I promise you that if we stop marijuana legalization, West Virginia will be a better place for it. Criminals will know that we have zero tolerance for any kind of drug in our state and they will pack up and leave. You personally will benefit from not having the temptation of weed around you. It will allow you to continue to focus on your studies and be the best student you can be. To benefit everyone in this room and everyone in our state, we must band together against legalization.

Applying the Skills of Critical Thinking

Brainstorm ways that you could enhance your ability to apply each of these critical thinking skills.

1. Questioning and challenging both your own ideas and the ideas of others.

2. Recognizing differences between ideas, between fact and opinion, explicit claims and unstated assumptions, and easily explained events and abnormalities or puzzles.

3. Forming opinions and supporting claims so that you can state and evaluate ideas.

4. Putting ideas into a broader context by seeing how the idea relates to what you already know and by understanding what they imply about other things you might assert or believe.

5. Critical judgments are those that you can articulate and defend by providing reasons for them. Why is it important to use the skills above to form critical judgments?

Name: _____   Section: _____   Time: _____

Identify the Rhetorical Techniques

Directions: After reviewing Martin Luther King's "I Have a Dream" speech, define the following rhetorical techniques. Insert and provide the definition along with an example from the speech.

1. Alliteration

2. Repetition

3. Parallelism

4. Analogy

5. Antithesis

6. Imagery

7. Concrete words

8. Abstract words

9. Rhythm

10. Simile

11. Metaphor

From *The Competent Communicator,* Second Edition, by Cristina Doda Cárdenas and Connie Duren. Copyright © 2013 by Kendall/Hunt Publishing Company. Reprinted by permission.

Criteria Used for Evaluating Speeches

The *average speech* (grade C) should meet the following criteria:

1. Conform to the kind of speech assigned—informative, persuasive, etc.
2. Be ready for presentation on the assigned date
3. Conform to the time limit
4. Fulfill any special requirements of the assignment—preparing an outline, using visual aids, conducting an interview, etc.
5. Have a clear specific purpose and central idea
6. Have an identifiable introduction, body, and conclusion
7. Show reasonable directness and competence in delivery
8. Be free of serious errors in grammar, pronunciation, and word usage

The *above average speech* (grade B) should meet the preceding criteria and also:

1. Deal with a challenging topic
2. Fulfill all major functions of a speech introduction and conclusion
3. Display clear organization of main points and supporting materials
4. Support main points with evidence that meets the tests of accuracy, relevance, objectivity, and sufficiency
5. Exhibit proficient use of connectives—transitions, internal previews, internal summaries, and signposts
6. Be delivered skillfully enough so as not to distract attention from the speaker's message

The *superior speech* (grade A) should meet all the preceding criteria and also:

1. Constitute a genuine contribution by the speaker to the knowledge or beliefs of the audience
2. Sustain positive interest, feeling, and/or commitment among the audience
3. Contain elements of vividness and special interest in the use of language
4. Be delivered in a fluent, polished manner that strengthens the impact of the speaker's message

The *below average speech* (grade D or F) is seriously deficient in the criteria required for the C speech.

Used with permission.

From *The Competent Communicator,* Second Edition, by Cristina Doda Cárdenas and Connie Duren. Copyright © 2013 by Kendall/Hunt Publishing Company. Reprinted by permission.

Speaking with Confidence: The Speaker

1. What distinguishes a reliable source from an unreliable one?

2. Explain why establishing credibility as a speaker is important.

3. What influence does appearance and language have on a speaker's credibility?

4. List the four dimensions of source credibility.

5. Does the same consideration of source credibility apply to debate and public speaking?

6. Briefly explain how a speaker can emphasize characteristic commonalities without sounding "fake."

7. What is the most important thing to remember about audience trust?

Name: _____   Section: _____   Time: _____

Exercise to Improve the Speaker's Nonverbal Communication

Objective: Review the criteria for each item and ask a peer to evaluate your performance.

Eye Contact

"An eye can threaten like a loaded and leveled gun; or can insult like hissing and kicking; or in its altered mood, by beams of kindness, making the heart dance with joy." (Emerson)

- Objective—Look sincerely and steadily at the speaker's audience.
- Evaluation

_____ **Yes** _____ **No**   Did the speaker maintain 85–95% eye contact with the audience?

_____ **Yes** _____ **No**   Did the speaker span the entire audience?

Posture/Movement/Gestures/Expression

"Stand tall. The difference between towering and cowering is totally a matter of inner posture. It's got nothing to do with height, it costs nothing, and it's more fun." (Malcomb Forbes)

- Objective—Make a good impression by looking confident while expressing energy.
- Evaluation

_____ **Yes** _____ **No**   Did the speaker initially smile at the audience?

_____ **Yes** _____ **No**   Did the speaker's face express interest in his/her topic/audience?

_____ **Yes** _____ **No**   Did the speaker tap his/her fingers or foot?

_____ **Yes** _____ **No**   Was the speaker's upper body posture erect?

_____ **Yes** _____ **No**   Did the speaker lean back on one hip while speaking?

_____ **Yes** _____ **No**   Did the speaker cross and uncross his/her legs while speaking?

_____ **Yes** _____ **No**   Was the speaker's movement purposeful?

From *The Competent Communicator,* Second Edition, by Cristina Doda Cárdenas and Connie Duren. Copyright © 2013 by Kendall/Hunt Publishing Company. Reprinted by permission.

Dress/Appearance

"The speaker never gets a second chance to make a first impression." (John Molloy)

◆   Objective: Good speakers know that they should dress one level nicer than their audience.
◆   Evaluation:

_____Yes   _____ No   Was the speaker dressed one level nicer than the audience?

_____Yes   _____ No   Was the speaker well groomed?

_____Yes   _____ No   Was the speaker wearing anything that was a distraction?

_____

Printed Name of Evaluator

_____

Signature of Evaluator

What Do I Wear for a Speech?

Do wear

- Appropriate clothing for the speech topic
- Clothes that fit (not oversized or too tight)
- Clothes that are clean and ironed
- Shirts (tucked in if designed to be)
- Shirts with sleeves
- Belt (if pants have belt loops)
- Shoes
- Hair away from eyes and face

Don't wear

- Clothes with tears or holes
- Low-cut jeans (we don't want to see your belly button or your boxer shorts)
- Short shorts or very short skirts
- Tops revealing midriff or cleavage
- Halter tops
- See-through tops
- T-shirts with logos, slogans, or irrelevant, distracting pictures/writing
- Outerwear (caps, hats, or coats)
- Sunglasses on your face or on top of your head
- Jewelry that is oversized, noisy, or clunky
- Distracting piercings
- Flip-flops or other very casual footwear

Cover up

- Large or distracting tattoos, if possible

Remember—Your appearance has a significant impact on your initial credibility. You may lose points on your speech grade if you dress inappropriately.

From *Experiences in Public Speaking,* Sixth Edition, by Marla D. Chisholm and Jackie Ganschow. Copyright © 2015 by Kendall Hunt Publishing Company. Reprinted by permission.

Name: _____   Section: _____   Time: _____

Exercises to Improve Vocal Delivery

Objective: Your voice is the primary vehicle for your message. Energy is transmitted through your voice and comes out as enthusiasm. Your vocal expression can be altered through exercises which impact relaxation, breathing, projection, and resonance.

Volume—The loudness or quietness of sound. It is possible to speak too loudly for a given audience, but most beginning speakers have the opposite problem. Some speakers speak too softly and cannot be heard in the back of the room.

  ◆ **Exercise**—Take a line from a poem, a song, or a limerick. Say the line so that the people in the first row can hear you. Next say the line so that the people in the second row can hear you. Keep repeating the line and projecting your voice further and further. Try this sentence: *"You never get a second chance to make a first impression."*

Emphasis—Varying the stress placed on words.
  ◆**Exercise**—Read each sentence emphasizing a different word each time.
    Now is the time for change
    Now **is** the time for change
    Now is **the** time for change
    Now is the **time** for change
    Now is the time **for** change
    Now is the time for **change**

Pitch—The highness or lowness of the speaker's voice. If pitch is not varied it will result in a monotone voice. You will sound so very dreary, boring, and sad.
  ◆ **Exercise**—Read the following James Joyce poem with appropriate pitch.
    The gray winds, the cold winds are blowing
    Where I go
    I hear the noise of many waters
    Far below
    All day, all night, I hear them flowing
    To and from

Rate—The speed at which a person speaks. Most people speak between 120 and 150 words per minute (wpm).
  ◆ **Exercise**—Try this nursery rhyme at several speeds.
    Piping hot, smoking hot
    What I've got, you have not

    See saw, Margery Daw
    Sold her bed and lay upon straw

Pause—A momentary break in the vocal delivery of the speech. It has been called an oral comma. Pause is used to signal the end of a thought, to give time for an idea to sink in, and to lend dramatic effect.

♦ **Exercise**— The following poem by Walt Whitman can be used for pitch, rate, and pause.

> O, captain, my captain, our fearful trip is done,
> The ship has weather'd every rack, the prize we sought is won,
> The port is near the bells I hear, the people all exulting,
> While fellow eyes the steady keel, the vessel grim and daring,
> But O heart! Heart! Heart!
> O the bleeding drops of red
> Where on my deck my captain lies
> Fallen cold and dead!

Pronunciation—The accepted standard of sound and rhythm for words in a given language.

♦ **Exercise**—Say the following words and then check the standard pronunciation for each word to see if you were correct.

- ➤ Library
- ➤ Hundred
- ➤ Athlete
- ➤ Relevant
- ➤ Strength
- ➤ Electoral
- ➤ Mischievous

Articulation—The physical production of particular speech sounds. Your goal is to speak words crisply and distinctly.

♦ **Exercise**—Can you translate the following articulation errors into standard English?

- ➤ Jeat yet
- ➤ Cannahepya
- ➤ Whadaydo
- ➤ Idunno
- ➤ Seeya
- ➤ fixinto

Colloquialism—Everyday speech common to a geographic area.

♦ **Exercise**—Can you translate what they mean to someone who speaks English as a second language?

- ➤ Apple of his eye
- ➤ Piece of cake
- ➤ Under the weather
- ➤ Whoop and holler
- ➤ Old as the hills
- ➤ Dumb as a rock
- ➤ Mad as a pot of collards
- ➤ Time is money
- ➤ It's raining cats and dogs

Speech Anxiety Coaching

We need to understand how our perceptions of the physiological reactions we experience in response to communication events (such as speeches) determine our interpretation of our communication ability. To a certain degree, everyone experiences the same neurobehavioral reactions when preparing to speak in front of an audience—it is how we interpret these feelings that matter.

Your instructor will pair you with a classmate. Ask the following questions:

When you experience speech anxiety, what are the underlying causes?

What uncertainties about public speaking tend to increase your feelings of self-doubt?

Now, pretend that you are coaching a person. First, acknowledge and validate the anxieties of this same person. Then, reviewing the strategies for building confidence in Chapter 2, make suggestions for each type of anxiety the same person faces.

Make sure you explain why you believe that strategy could be effective in helping reduce the specific anxiety. (Example: Your classmate says she feels "terrified" in the moments before beginning a speech. You acknowledge that these feelings are normal and that it is a chemical reaction in the brain. Then you suggest that he or she should realize the same chemical reactions occur in everyone in a similar situation to a certain degree, and that adrenaline could be relabeled as "excitement"—like the excitement one feels before playing in a big sporting event that they enjoy).

Coach and be coached by your classmates—we are all in this together!

Reflecting on the Spotlight Effect
and Illusion of Transparency

The spotlight effect leads a speaker to think that people observe him or her much more carefully than they actually do. Many speakers also experience the illusion of transparency, believing that their internal states, such as speech anxiety, are easily visible to the audience. Overall, we tend to be our own worst critic. How can we break free from the spotlight effect and illusion of transparency? This chapter discusses a lot of strategies; many of these suggest focusing on your audience. I would also like you to consider yourself as an audience member for this discussion.

When you are an audience, what type of person are you? Think of a recent situation when you were an audience listening to a speaker. Were you highly critical of the speaker? Did you judge him or her harshly for any type of error he or she committed? Do you remember every mistake he or she made?

Now, describe what you believe is a typical audience member for a professional presentation. Do you believe that the typical peer is hypercritical and judgmental of you? Do you think your peers care more about your presentation or their presentation? Do they give you their complete attention, looking for mistakes and ways to judge you?

Finally, what does this type of exercise lead you to think about the next time you give a presentation? How can you use the ideas of the spotlight effect and illusion of transparency to lower our communication anxiety? Discuss how you can relabel your perceptions of your audience to manage speech anxiety, build confidence, and improve your effectiveness when you speak.

Name: _____   Section: _____   Time: _____

Recognizing PowerPoint DOs and DON'Ts

Objective

To learn and identify requirements for the creation of a PowerPoint slide show to be utilized as a visual aid for a speech presentation.

Instructions

1. Your instructor will tell you how to access the PowerPoint DOs and DON'Ts slide shows.
2. **Choose any three of the slide shows to view.** While/after viewing each slide show, answer the questions on the next page. You will be identifying the "DOs and DON'Ts" of using PowerPoint as a visual aid in a speech. (Each slide show will have more than three weaknesses and three strengths.) If you have difficulty identifying three of the requirements followed and three of the requirements violated, you should choose another slide show to view.

In order to correctly identify the requirements followed and violated, you will need to refer to the information covered in class for computer-generated visual aids and the "PowerPoint Requirements" provided on the page following this assignment. Understand that you will not receive credit if your responses to do not reference *specific* PowerPoint requirements.

Examples of DOs/DON'Ts that WILL receive credit:
"The font colors for titles and text are consistent throughout the slide show."
"There is correct grammar and spelling on all slides."
"The picture on slide #5 is too small to be seen by audience members in the back of the room."
"There is no blank slide at the end of the presentation."

Examples of DOs/DON'Ts that WILL NOT receive credit:
"Pretty picture."
"Just the right amount of slides."
"Crazy transitions."
"Too many words."

From *Experiences in Public Speaking,* Sixth Edition, by Marla D. Chisholm and Jackie Ganschow. Copyright © 2015 by Kendall Hunt Publishing Company. Reprinted by permission.

A Public Speaking Delivery Checklist

◆ Avoid off-the-topic comments as you approach the stage and before you begin your speech.
◆ Be aware of social fillers: "uhs . . . ums . . . you know . . . like . . . erh . . . whatever . . ."
◆ Find friendly faces in the audience, make eye contact, and scan the room slowly. Find the individuals in the audience who are giving you positive feedback then connect with them.
◆ Let your hands fall gracefully to your sides and make natural gestures. Avoid crossing your hands in front of or behind you, stuffing your hands in your pockets, and pacing in front of the audience.
◆ Never apologize regardless of the situation!
◆ Pause before you begin your speech. Make eye-contact with those in your audience.
◆ Take a deep breath, exhale, and smile before you begin speaking.
◆ Upon conclusion of your speech, pause, make eye contact, and allow the audience a few moments to reflect upon your presentation before returning quietly to your seat.

From *The Competent Communicator,* Second Edition, by Cristina Doda Cárdenas and Connie Duren. Copyright © 2013 by Kendall/Hunt Publishing Company. Reprinted by permission.

Unethical Behavior: Determining Plagiarism and Cheating

Objective

To recognize unethical behavior when it occurs in a Public Speaking course.

Instructions

After reading about the three different kinds of plagiarism, analyze the situations given below and decide if the students have committed plagiarism or have cheated. If you think the students have plagiarized, identify which kind of plagiarism they committed. Be able to defend your decisions orally.

To **plagiarize** is to present another person's language or ideas as your own—to give the impression that you have written or thought of something yourself when you have actually taken it from someone else.

Global plagiarism: stealing an entire speech or assignment

Patchwork plagiarism: stealing ideas or language from two or three sources

Incremental plagiarism: failing to give credit for particular parts or increments of a speech that are borrowed from other people (quotes or paraphrases)

1. Anna buys an entire speech from an online source, writes it on note cards, and then delivers it as if it were her own work. *Anna (has) (has not) plagiarized. Reasons?*

2. On the Internet, Aiden finds an outline of a speech about college students and stress. He adds one additional example to the speech, but otherwise does not change it. Aiden then presents the speech in class as his own. *Aiden (has) (has not) plagiarized. Reasons?*

3. Ruben and Matthew are in two different Public Speaking sections. They work together on a speech on the topic of "How the Pyramids Were Built." They share the same sources: two Internet sources and a book. They write the speech together and prepare identical outlines. Each gives essentially the same speech in his class. *Ruben and Matthew (have) (have not) cheated. Reasons?*

4. Vivian uses statistics extensively in her speech on medical waste which washes up on local beaches, but she does not tell her audience the sources of her statistics. *Vivian (has) (has not) plagiarized. Reasons?*

5. Together, Monica and Alex watch two instructional DVDs in the SCC. Monica completes the worksheets that accompany the DVDs, but Alex doesn't find the time. He copies Monica's worksheets and turns them in for credit. *Alex (has) (has not) plagiarized. Monica (has) (has not) cheated. Reasons?*

6. Together, Becky and Audrey watch two instructional DVDs in the SCC. After watching the recordings, they work together on the worksheets that accompany the DVDs. They turn in identical worksheets. *Becky and Audrey (have) (have not) cheated. Reasons?*

7. Together, Jack and David watch two instructional DVDs in the SCC. After watching the DVDs, they discuss the answers to the worksheets that accompany the recordings. Later that day, each one individually completes the worksheets. *Jack and David (have) (have not) cheated. Reasons?*

8.   Ian's class is expected to watch a recorded speech in the SCC and write a critique on the speech. Ian doesn't watch the speech, but his friend Marco does. Ian takes Marco's critique and rewrites it. Ian makes sure to vary the sentence structure and the wording so that the critique is not identical to Marco's.*Ian (has) (has not) plagiarized. Marco(has) (has not) cheated. Reasons?*

9.   Amanda finds three articles online that each offer unique information about her speech topic. She uses pieces of all three articles when she writes her speech. The day of her speech she does not cite any of these sources, although she does cite some other sources from which she gathered information.*Amanda (has) (has not) plagiarized. Reasons?*

10. Leslie and Reid, who are in different Public Speaking classes, are working in the SCC on an assignment that requires them to make a slide show for a PowerPoint presentation. Leslie doesn't know much about PowerPoint, so Reid helps her. He explains how to download photos and shows her a picture he has downloaded from the Internet that he intends to use for his assignment. Interestingly, Leslie realizes that this same picture would be appropriate for her presentation also. She downloads the identical picture and uses it in her slide show. *Leslie (has) (has not) cheated. Reasons?*

11. Jose and Sarah are in the same Public Speaking class. Jose finds an Internet source that has interesting information for Sarah's topic area. He gives Sarah the web address, and she gets valuable information from the site. Sarah uses the source in her speech even though she did not find it on her own.*Jose and Sarah (have) (have not) cheated. Reasons?*

12. Lillian, Noah, Ramesh, and Courtney form a study group. When a take-home test is distributed in their Public Speaking class, all four of the students make sure they have read the chapters and studied for the test. At a set time, they meet to collaboratively take the test.*The students in the study group (have) (have not) cheated. Reasons?*

Free Speech and Productive Communication

Should speakers on college campuses be allowed to choose any topic they wish? Or should some topics be off-limits? How do you balance free expression, pursuing justice, and promoting a productive communication climate?

Next, think about our class. What topics, if any, do you think students should not be allowed to speak on? Justify your position. Please explicitly reference the concepts of <u>communication climate</u> and <u>dialogue</u> in your justification.

Listening and Speech Analysis Exercise

Your instructor will play a speech in the class for you to analyze.

Identify one specific example of each of the following concepts from Chapter 1:

Logos-

Pathos-

Ethos-

Mythos-

Then, I would like you to discuss your ability to listen. Why were you able or not able to listen effectively to this speech? Please discuss how <u>distractions</u>, <u>listening anxiety</u>, and <u>personal judgment</u> either facilitated or inhibited your ability to listen effectively to this speech.

Distractions-

Listening Anxiety-

Personal Judgment-

Name: _____   Section: _____   Time: _____

Identifying Your Speech Objectives
(Planning Tools)

Directions: You should complete the planning tools before you research your speech. You will need to submit this document on the day of the workshop.

1. **Topic:**

2. **Title:**

3. **General Purpose (broad goal):**
    _____ to inform
    _____ to persuade
    _____ to entertain

4. **Specific Purpose (precise goal with your audience):** You can start with "to inform my audience about" or "after listening to my speech my audience will."

5. **Central Idea/Preview/Thesis (what you want your audience to remember from your speech in one complete sentence):** Your audience should be able to identify the unifying idea / theme / thread that runs throughout your speech.

From *The Competent Communicator,* Second Edition, by Cristina Doda Cárdenas and Connie Duren. Copyright © 2013 by Kendall/Hunt Publishing Company. Reprinted by permission.

Name: _____   Section: _____   Time: _____

Critical Analysis: Speeches

Instructions: In this class, everyone is a teacher and everyone is a learner. The purpose is to get students familiar with teaching content to others. First, divide the class into seven groups and each group will discuss a specific form of communication. For instance, Group 1: Nonverbal Communication; Group 2: Small Group Communication; Group 3: Communication in Organizations (Business Communication); Group 4: Interpersonal Communication; Group 5: Intercultural Communication; Group 6: Mass Media; and Group 7: Communication and Technology

Each group will be responsible for choosing a topic related to their specific communicative genre. The goal is not to teach the textbook, but is to further investigate on a specific topic. There is one lesson plan per group and all members will receive the same grade for the outline and presentation. Each group's packet must include:

- One grading rubric, lesson plan, and reference page.
- The rough draft portion of the outline for each individual's portion of the presentation.
- A list of three engaging and thought provoking discussion questions relating to your presentation. In addition, there must be a detailed explanation of the goal or purpose behind each question. These three questions will also need to be posted on the online discussion board.
- During the presentation, the group must use some type of visual aid, other than Power-Point. The groups can use video clips, posters, audio, the class, a dynamic or intriguing discussion question, a game, or a hand out. The group must find some way to create an interactive learning installation that engages the class.

The group will then present their lesson to the class. Lessons should be 25–30 minutes. Further, the presentations and teaching packets should follow the following format:

Topic:

Teaching Objectives:
(What is your goal? What do you want the audience walking away knowing? Basically, what is the main message of this lesson).

Teaching Materials:
(Please state any materials that will be needed in order to complete the assignment. For instance, any hand-outs, video clips, props, etc.)
Discussion Questions: (Please make sure to use grammatically, correct sentences).

1. State Discussion Question 1 and the goal.
2. State Discussion Question 2 and the goal.
3. State Discussion Question 3 and the goal.

From *Workbook for Public Speaking in Everyday Life,* Second Edition, by Jennifer A. Marshall. Copyright © 2017 by Kendall Hunt Publishing Company. Reprinted by permission.

<u>Title of Your Lesson Plan</u>
THIS IS WHERE YOUR GROUP WILL START THE PRESENTATION

I.   Introduction
       A. Attention Getter

       B. Thesis

       C. Credibility

       D. Preview of Main Points:

           1. Background Information;

           2. The New Insights;

           3. Teaching Installation.

II.   Body (Make sure to use a full sentence starting with a transitional word).
       A. Background Information (Your specific background information will depend
           on your topic and scope. These are just ideas and you are welcome to add your
           own).

           1. Provide the necessary background information.

           2. Discuss the broad genre.

           3. Place your new insight into a specific context.

           4. Is there any historical information that the audience should know/?

      5. Are there any laws influencing this form of communication?

      6. What are the norms?

B. The New Insight (A full sentence transition is required).

      1. This is where you providing new insight into your communicative genre.

          a. Make sure to get specific and cite sources.

          b. This is not where any textbook material should be presented.

          c. Your goal is to expand the audience's scope on your specific genre

      2. You should be spending at least 15 minutes in this section expanding on the concepts.

C. The Teaching Installation: (Full sentence transition required).

      1. This is where you conduct some type of activity with the class.

      2. This can be an analytical, writing, listening, or even speaking activity the class has to physical do. You can even do multiple activities.

      3. All the activities should be reinforcing the topics brought up in the previous section.

      4. In addition, to the activity you must debrief with the class.

        a. In this debrief, you should discuss with the class if they know why they had you do the activity?

        b. You should be testing to see if they understood and were able to articulate similar goals.

        c. If the audience has a difference opinion, discuss the group's purpose for the activity.

III.   Conclusion: (Full sentence transition required).
      A. Re-cap (Restate your three main points).

        1. Main point 1

        2. Main point 2

        3. Main point 3

      B. Call to Action: (Challenge the audience to do something related to your communicative genre).

      C. Ending Grabber

      Followed by alphabetized references stated in APA or MLA.

Individual Teaching Installation:

In addition, each individual person will be responsible for typing up a one to two page reflection paper. This paper will be due the class after their presentation. Examine the group dynamics, the work you completed for the project, and evaluate your performance in the group. Each member will receive an individual grade for this portion of the assignment.

Persuasive Audience Analysis

Speech Topic: (By the end of my speech, I want to persuade my audience to . . .)

_____

_____

Audience Attitudes

Place a hash mark (/) on the blank after the term that best explains your current feelings toward this topic.

Hostile

I am moderately to strongly against this topic.

_____

Apathetic

I do not really have strong feelings for or against this topic.

_____

Friendly

I am moderately or strongly in favor of this topic.

_____

- -

If you have a **hostile** audience, then you will need to concentrate on justifying why your plan is better than the other side's plan. For example, you need to be able to explain that legalizing the use of marijuana is a better course of action than making marijuana illegal. (If you have a hostile audience, you might focus on the arguments/reasons you give in your speech on trying to get people to change their attitudes.)

If you have an **apathetic** audience, then you need to focus your speech on explaining why your topic is important to the audience. You need to motivate the audience to care. (With an apathetic audience, you might focus the arguments/reasons you give in your speech on getting your audience to change their attitude and, perhaps, their behavior.)

If you have a **friendly** audience, then you need to concentrate on making your audience feel more strongly about your topic. For instance, if your audience agrees that voting is important, then you should concentrate your efforts on getting people to go out and vote. (Since your audience already "agrees" you might want to use arguments/reasons in your speech aimed at getting people to act.)

Stealing or Just Borrowing? An Inference and Fact Exercise

Directions: Answer the following questions. Based on the story below, are the following statements, True, False or not known. Mark the appropriate answer. The question mark represents the not known answer choice.

> A homeowner had just turned off the lights in their living room when a woman appeared and demanded something of value. The owner opened the wall safe. The contents of the wall safe were taken and the woman left. The police were called immediately. When the police arrived they noticed the window was open.

True   False   ?

❏ ❏ ❏   1. A woman appeared after the homeowner had turned off the lights.

❏ ❏ ❏   2. The thief was a woman.

❏ ❏ ❏   3. The thief did not demand money.

❏ ❏ ❏   4. The person who opened the wall safe was the home owner.

❏ ❏ ❏   5. The homeowner took what was in the wall safe and left the house.

❏ ❏ ❏   6. A person opened the wall safe.

❏ ❏ ❏   7. The woman and the homeowner live in the house together as a married couple.

❏ ❏ ❏   8. Do we know how much money was in the wall safe?

❏ ❏ ❏   9. The thief demanded money from the homeowner?

❏ ❏ ❏   10. The story mentions only three persons: the homeowner, the woman who demanded something of value and the police.

From *The Competent Communicator,* Second Edition, by Cristina Doda Cárdenas and Connie Duren. Copyright © 2013 by Kendall/Hunt Publishing Company. Reprinted by permission.

Oral Citations Activity

Directions

With your group members, create an oral citation for each of the sources in the following, using the information provided. Then, present the oral citations to the class as a group.

Source 1

Book: *Global Warming: The Causes and Consequences*
Date of Publication: Dec 23, 2010
Publisher: Mind Melodies
Excerpt:

> "An increase in global temperature will cause sea levels to rise and will change the amount and pattern of precipitation, probably including expansion of subtropical deserts. Warming is expected to be highest in the Arctic and would be associated with continuing retreat of glaciers, permafrost and sea ice."

Author: Ishita Haldar

Source 2

Last Updated: July 11, 2016
Source: www.cdc.gov
Title: *Children in the Home*
Excerpt:

> "Although secondhand smoke exposure among children has dropped over the past 15 years, children are still more heavily exposed to secondhand smoke than adults. About two in five U.S. children aged 3–11 years (40.6%) are exposed to secondhand smoke. In the United States, the percentage of children and teens living with at least one smoker is about three times the percentage of nonsmoking adults who live with a smoker. Making your home and vehicles smoke-free can reduce secondhand smoke exposure among children and nonsmoking adults. Some studies indicate that these rules can also help smokers quit and can reduce adolescents' risk of becoming smokers."

Source: Centers for Disease Control and Prevention

Source 3

Date: July 2016
Publication: Journal of Policy Practice
Title: *Policy Implementation Under Class Action-Based Reform of State Child Welfare Agencies: The Cases of Washington State and New Jersey*

> **Excerpt:** "Increasingly, child welfare advocates have turned to class action lawsuits to improve child protective and foster care services of state child welfare agencies.

The litigation process involves identifying agency deficiencies and specifying in a negotiated and court-approved settlement agreement performance improvements required to resolve the lawsuit. The challenge for agency leaders is to develop and implement new policies and strategies to achieve performance improvements within a bureaucratic social services system operating under conditions of unlimited demand and limited resources"

Source/Author: Ariel Alvarez, Assistant Professor of Child Advocacy and Policy at Montclair State University

Source 4

Last Updated: January 22, 2016
Source: www.cancer.org

> **Excerpt:** "A risk factor is anything that affects your chance of getting a disease such as cancer. Different cancers have different risk factors. Lifestyle-related risk factors such as body weight, physical activity, diet, and tobacco use, play a major role in many adult cancers. But these factors usually take many years to influence cancer risk, and they are not thought to play much of a role in childhood cancers, including neuroblastomas."

Source: American Cancer Society

Source 5

Book: *Social Media: Usage and Impact*
Date of Publication: Dec 16, 2011
Publisher: Lexington Books
Excerpt:

"Facebook initially allowed only college students to become members, and remains the most popular social medium among college students. In a recent study, college students were reported to be using Facebook approximately 30 min throughout the day as part of their daily routine. Facebook expanded to allow any member of the public to join, and now reports more internet traffic than any other social media in the United States."

Source/Author: Hana S. Noor Al-Deen (Professor of Communication at University of North Carolina) and John Allen Hendricks

Source 6

Find your own source online, and create an oral citation from it.

TOPIC	FACT	ORAL CITATION	OPINION	ORAL CITATION
Abortion				
Assisted Suicide				
Banning Books				
Corporal Punishment				
Human Trafficking				
Legalization of Marijuana				

Paraphrasing

Defined

The process of paraphrasing (active listening) involves the restating a speaker's thoughts and/or feelings in the your own words. It is your interpretation of the speaker's message. The skill of paraphrasing demonstrates:

- **Attentiveness and listening ability**
  - ➤ Does not miss any of the speaker's comments
  - ➤ Does not plan what to say next while the speaker is talking
- **The ability to avoid judgmental language**
  - ➤ Does not insert his/her own perception
  - ➤ Does not assign fault or blame

Method

1. Change the speaker's wording.
2. Offer an example of what you think the speaker is talking about.
3. Reflect the underlying theme of the speaker's remarks.

Practical Application

Rewrite the following statements.
1. "It's not fair that I have to work so much. Other students can get better grades because they have time to study."
2. "You'll have the best chance of getting a loan for the new car you want if you give us a complete financial statement and credit history.
3. "They haven't called me in ages. I think they must be mad at me or something."
4. "Why don't you try to be less messy around here? This place looks like a dump!"

Creating Oral Citations for Your Speech

As research is the skeleton of your presentation, you should be sure to cite your research throughout. You will not receive an appreciable grade on your presentation if you use few or no research citations in the body of your presentation; and, in fact, a presentation without any source citations indicates you have plagiarized the material and thus you could receive an F. So, doing the actual research is only half the battle in doing a presentation; much of that research should be incorporated into the presentation itself through citations.

Tips on using citations within your speech:

From a reference work: Work, credentials, and date

The 2011 edition of Simmons Market Research, considered by many to be the most comprehensive source for market data, notes that automobiles produced after the government bailout are more fuel efficient, and advertising has emphasized such improvements.

From a book: Author, brief credentials (if applicable), title

Dr. David Schwartz, dean of the biology department of Princeton University, wrote in his 2016 book "*Evolution Awry*," that the genetic anomalies found in these island inhabitants illustrate their connection to their mainland ancestors.

From a website: Site and last update

The Consumer Reports website, last updated in December 2016, states that consumers prefer the Whirlpool brand 2 to 1 over all other brands.

From a TV Show: Name of the show and date

On a show that was aired in December 2014, 60 Minutes reported that 21 of the survivors have repeated the trip made on the anniversary of the tragedy.

From an interview you performed: Name, credentials, date

"February 20th, I spoke with Charlotte Maddux, Director of the local chapter of the American Red Cross, who told me that the tri-state area averages for blood donations fell by 30 percent last year."
From an interview not performed by you: Name, date, interview source, credentials
Appearing on the television program, "Dateline," on February 5, 2017, noted psychologist Dr. Michael Beck of Harvard University argued that victimization, while not always necessary before a violent act, is the single strongest predictor.

From a publication: Name, credentials, publication, date

White House Chief of Staff George Stephanopoulos, asserted in the January 30, 2000 edition of the *Wall Street Journal* that President Clinton was the driving force for the welfare to work legislation, not the conservative dominated congress.
**You should NOT give the information and then say, ". . . and that was according to . . .." At that point, the information has passed and the citation can confuse the audience rather than strengthen your ethos.

Selecting a Topic for Your Speeches

For this class, you are asked to pick the same topic for both your informative and persuasive speeches. Each student should select a <u>different civic topic</u>. Merriam-Webster Dictionary defines civic as "of or relating to a citizen, a city, citizenship, or community affairs." In the first speech on your topic, you will be asked to inform the audience about a civic issue. In the persuasive speech, you will be asked to present an argument for a potential solution to address an area of the civic issue that needs improvement.

STEP 1: Brainstorm a list of topics that would interest you and your audience.

STEP 2: Select two topics from the list to analyze further. Evaluate each of your potential topics using the criteria listed in our textbook (your own interests, the audience, resource availability, the time limits, and the setting and occasion). Examine each of your potential topics for their opportunities and constraints. Keep in mind that both speeches should be of less than 10 min.

STEP 3: Based on this analysis, select one of the potential topics as your potential civic topic for this course. For your first speech, your general purpose is to inform. Write a specific purpose for your hypothetical topic for the first speech. Then, write a thesis statement that would be appropriate for an informative speech on this topic.

The Process of Researching Your Topic

First, list your topic, your specific purpose for the informative speech, and your thesis statement for the informative speech.

Next, give an overview of the sources you consulted on this topic. Tell us specifically how you used the resources within the Marshall University library website to gather information for your topic. You are welcome to create this as a bulleted list. I expect to read about at least five different options within the library website that you referred.

Then, briefly discuss what is going on well in your research process and what questions you have that are still unanswered. Are you struggling to find the information you need? What questions do you have at this point? If you feel confident, then say so. If you have questions, please ask now.

Finally, after looking at the quality of the information about this topic, what do you think should be the main ideas or subtopics that you cover in your speech? We are going to call these as the main points and start talking about how to construct the body of your speech next week. For now, what ideas or concepts seem to be important enough to warrant becoming the main idea of your speech? You are not promising that these will be your main ideas; I just want to see what potential main topics you are considering after doing some research. Your main points are meant to help focus on your research as well.

Locating Supporting Material

DIRECTIONS:

Use the Marshall University (MU) Library databases to find all types of supporting material. Gather the information and present it in your own words. Then, explain why you think this is quality information. Provide the reference for each type of supporting material.

TOPIC:

THESIS STATEMENT DRAFT:

SUPPORTING MATERIAL

1. EXAMPLE
   a. Paraphrased Information
   b. Please explain how this example is both concrete and generalizable.
   c. MLA/APA Reference

2. DEFINITION
   a. Paraphrased Information
   b. Please explain how well your definition clarifies the topic.
   c. MLA/APA Reference

3. TESTIMONY
   a. Paraphrased Information
   b. Please explain how the testimony is free of bias (or how you explicitly mention potential bias); the credibility of the source; and the expertise (education + experience of the course).
   c. MLA/APA Reference

4. FACT OR STATISTIC
   a. Paraphrased Information
   b. Please explain how this fact or statistic is RECENT, free from bias, and easy for your audience to comprehend.
   c. MLA/APA Reference

Name: _____   Section: _____   Time: _____

Developing a Bibliography/Work Cited and Note Cards

Instructions: Complete your bibliography/work cited using either MLA or APA format. Check with your instructor for their format preference. Each citation should include the authors name, year of publication, title, and publisher. Next, complete your notecards on 3 x 5 ruled cards. Attach your cards to this document for review. Remember to keep your notes brief and number your cards.

Bibliography/Work Cited:

Document Your Sources on Your Written Outline

List all your sources in alphabetical order on your planning and outline document. Use MLA or APA format.

- Go online (alltheweb.com; sourceaid.com; gosource.com).
- Search for the exact term *MLA Style Manual*
- Follow the instructions for keying in your source and your final credit will look something like this:
  - Fritsch, Jane. "Evidence of innocence can come too late for freedom." *The New York Times* 30 July 2000 (p. WK-3 in original publication). Available online (*www.nytimes.com*). Retrieved 4 Feb. 2001.

Note Cards (Xerox and staple a copy of your note cards to this page):

Name: _____   Section: _____   Time: _____

Exercise on Ethical Research and Speaking

Purpose

To apply skills learned in lecture and readings about plagiarism and public speaking.
Instructions: Using personal knowledge, library and electronic research sources, complete the following questions.

> Vice President Joseph Biden (2009) was forced to withdraw his candidacy from the 1988 presidential race because of an act of questionable ethics in public speaking. In more than one instance, it was discovered that Senator Biden (D-Del) had used, directly and with some paraphrase, the words of others in his speeches.

1. Whose words did Biden steal in the campaign scandal?

2. Have there been other instances of plagiarism in Biden's life? If so, describe the circumstance.

3. Using APA/MLA format, list the sources of your information.

Organizational Patterns

Instructions: Fill in the blank with the appropriate letter of your response. Rewrite sentence #5 and #8 using parallel sentence structure.

A. Spatial
B. Topical
C. Causal
D. Chronological
E. Problem-Solution

_____ 1. There are four sequential steps in getting a professional tattoo.

_____ 2. The Eiffel Tower is divided into three sections.

_____ 3. The problem of using aging planes by U.S. airline companies threatens the safety of air travel.

_____ 4. The causes for the collapse of the Mayan civilization have not been fully explained.

_____ 5. Today's talk will be about achieving my childhood dreams, helping others to achieve their childhood dreams, and the lessons learned in the process.

_____ 6. The story of Picasso's life can be discussed by examining his talents as a painter, sculptor, and printmaker.

_____ 7. Pet therapy has been found to decrease loneliness and improve physical health in nursing home patients.

_____ 8. As we travel through the world of tomatoes, we will look at different varieties, answer the question is it fruit or vegetable and share some of the uses.

_____ 9. The major kinds of fireworks are skyrockets, Roman candles, pinwheels, and lances.

_____ 10. Giving directions is easy if you follow these four easy steps.

Name: _____   Section: _____   Time: _____

Writing the Introduction

Directions: Your job in the introduction is to capture the audience's attention, give them any background information they need, motivate them to listen, establish your own credibility, and preview what is to come. You can arrange the background information, motivation/benefit statement, and credibility statement in any order you please. Please remember attention material is always first and the preview to the body and transition is always last.

1. **Attention**
   a. Choose one of the following techniques:
      _____ story
      _____ startling statement
      _____ quotation
      _____ rhetorical question
      _____ illustration
      _____ humorous story
      _____ statistic
   b. State your attention statement below:

2. **Background Information**
   a. If the audience will need a brief statement or definition to help them understand your speech you will need to include this step.
   b. State your background statement below:

3. **Motivation/Benefit Statement**
   a. You are to give your audience a reason to listen which will motivate them to listen to your speech.
   b. State your motivation/benefit statement below:

4. **Credibility Statement**
    a. You can meet this objective by
        1) Revealing the sources you reviewed
        2) Expressing your connection to the topic
    b. State your credibility statement below:

5. **Preview/Transition to Body**
    a. Use your central idea (thesis) as a preview to the body.
    b. Smoothly transition to the first main point of the body.

Name: _____   Section: _____   Time: _____

Writing the Conclusion

Directions: Your job is to develop a conclusion that will signal the end, summarize what has been said, and end by referring back to the introduction or with a sense of finality/impact.

1. Signal the end (this can be accomplished with a transitional phrase)
    State your statement below:

2. Summarize or review your main points (thesis)
    State your statement below:

3. Tie your conclusion to the introduction
    State your statement below:

4. Provide closure by ending with impact or sense of finality (the techniques you used in the attention statement may work here)
    State your statement below:

Use Signposts and Transitional Phrases
to Create Flow and Cohesion

Elements that show additional detail	Elements that show cause and effect
◆ Moreover ◆ Furthermore ◆ Further ◆ Additionally ◆ In addition to ◆ Besides ◆ Also ◆ Again ◆ Another	◆ Accordingly ◆ Therefore ◆ For this reason ◆ Thus ◆ So ◆ As a result ◆ Consequently
Elements that show comparisons	**Elements that show contrast**
◆ Similarly ◆ Likewise ◆ In comparison ◆ Here again	◆ However ◆ As opposed to ◆ But ◆ Yet ◆ Although
Elements that illustrate	**Elements that show time and order**
◆ For example ◆ In particular ◆ For instance ◆ This means ◆ In other words	◆ First, second, third ◆ Finally ◆ Subsequently ◆ Before, after ◆ Previously ◆ Next
Elements that summarize	**Now, make a list of your own:**
◆ In brief ◆ In short ◆ In conclusion ◆ Finally ◆ To sum it up ◆ In closing ◆ One final thought	

Strategies for Persuading about Problems

1. Show the problem is current and demands immediate attention, as well as being in need of a quick solution. The problem must be important and part of a larger, ongoing problem.
2. Prove the problem is individualistic or part of a community, state, nation, or world. The problem must impact international science, as well as a community, state, and nation.
3. The public is aware of the problem or is beginning to show an awareness of the problem.
4. The problem is in the development stage, and, if not recognized, will continue to worsen.
5. With the problem impacts expansion or improvement of human conditions or health. Survival, physical existence, and security are representative of the problem.
6. Investigate the relevance of political, social, economic, religious, or moral issues of the problem.
7. Define the specific cause(s) underlying the problem.
8. People involved are humiliated, threatened, or tormented by the problem.
9. Connect with the audience to prove the problem could affect them. Those affected have the same values and needs as the audience.
10. Show society's failure to acknowledge the problem will result in harm.
11. The problem interferes with the audience's plans, objectives, or ambitions.
12. The problem harms or affects the audience directly or indirectly. The problem prevents a society or individual from moving forward.
13. Show how the problem impacts individuals, groups, or societies.
14. Show the problem interferes with production in societies or institutions.
15. Show harm has previously occurred to the audience because of an identical problem.
16. Show the infrastructure, employees, or programs are defunct because of the problem.
17. Show the problem creates or leads to future problems.
18. Prove the problem is of high importance—more so than other problems. Show our adversaries benefit from the problem.
19. The problem is acknowledged by community, state, national, or world leaders.
20. Show society is conflicted in its views and beliefs regarding the problem.

From *The Competent Communicator,* Second Edition, by Cristina Doda Cárdenas and Connie Duren. Copyright © 2013 by Kendall/Hunt Publishing Company. Reprinted by permission.

Strategies for Persuading about Solutions

1. Show the solution will decrease or eliminate the source of the problem by dealing with the underlying causes.
2. Show the symptoms of the problem will decrease or eliminate the reoccurring symptoms of the problem.
3. Even though the causes of the problem may be anonymous or debated, examine two advantages which target the symptoms that can be easily and quickly applied.
4. Find an analogy to use as an example of how the problem has successfully been solved or dealt with elsewhere. Persuade the audience to agree with you.
5. If possible, show the audience the solution(s) have achieved success in diverse situations and will continue to work in all situations/places.
6. Establish credibility by using professional/expert testimony supporting basic principles and concrete procedures.
7. Give many alternatives to the solution(s). Be logical and specific. Show solution(s) that have and have not worked. State your personal choice and the reasons why the solution will work.
8. Motivate the audience to accept your solution(s) by removing any barriers.
9. Prove to the audience they will feel more satisfied if they put your solution(s) into place.
10. Show how your solution will fulfill the needs of the audience, and how unsatisfied the audience may be if change does not occur.
11. Show the audience the solution is representative of their values, standards, principles, and beliefs—your solution is symbolic of the masses of people.
12. Show the solution is in contrast to lowered values and will not infringe upon basic rights.
13. Show the audience why they should adopt your solution(s) quickly.
14. Show the audience their current methods are outdated and adopting new proposals will increase success.
15. To avoid conflicts, rephrase the audience's values that are violated.
16. Lead the audience through visualization to picture the outcome if your solution(s) are adopted. Show the alternative consequences.
17. Show that implementation of the new solution(s) will have a positive outcome. Show the positive results outweigh the negative results, and the problem can be resolved. Show that following the current course or path will result in more negative consequences.
18. Show the audience how to implement the solution(s). Make sure the audience understands the steps that must be taken.
19. Anticipate arguments against your solution(s) by having researched the topic and by using credible sources to reinforce your ideas.
20. Be specific and detailed, and show the solution(s) are well researched.
21. Show the solution(s) can be put into operation—they are sensible, possible, realistic, and economical.
22. Show partial changes will not suffice, and complete changes are needed.
23. Prove your solution(s) are uphold the law and constitution.

From *The Competent Communicator,* Second Edition, by Cristina Doda Cárdenas and Connie Duren. Copyright © 2013 by Kendall/Hunt Publishing Company. Reprinted by permission.

24.   Explain any changes needed in laws or constitutions and the majority needed for change to occur.
25.   Show the general public and your supports back your solution(s).
26.   Began explaining your solution(s) by revealing those facts most appealing to your audience then disclose the more controversial points.
27.   Motivate the audience to implement your solution(s) causing change by appealing to their values, beliefs, wants, and needs.

Traditional: Speeches

Refutation Pattern of Arrangement:

The goal of this persuasive format is to debate the opposition's stance. The speaker's goal is to disprove or refute the opposition's claims. This organization works best with hostile audiences, who disagree with your stance. Often, this pattern is used in political campaigns.

Title

I.   Introduction

    A. Attention

    B. Thesis

    C. Credibility

    D. Preview

        1.

        2.

        3.

        4.

II.   Body (Full sentence transition required)

    A. The Opposition
        1. State the opposing claims

        2.

        3.

    B. Implication of opposing claims (Full sentence transition required)
        1. Ramifications of the opposition

        2.

        3.

    C. Speaker's position arguments
        1.

        2.

        3.

    D. Contrast
        1. Contrast your claims with the oppositional stance

        2. Re-expose the major flaws in the oppositional stance

        3. Drive home the speaker's stance showing why it is superior

III.   Conclusion (Full sentence transition required)
    A. Recap
        1.

        2.

        3.

        4.

    B. Call to Action

    C. Ending Grabber

References in APA or MLA to follow.

Informative Speech

For your first major presentation this semester, you must prepare and deliver a 5–7 min informative speech **that focuses on a civic issue**. You may want to discuss a civic topic that relates to your major. For example, a nursing major may discuss the controversy surrounding stem cell research, a preeducation major may explain objections to standardized testing, or a business major may explain how a minimum wage influences the economy. You should consider selecting a topic that is <u>also appropriate for a persuasive speech</u> later in the semester.

This speech gives you the opportunity to demonstrate what you have learned about selecting and researching a topic, organizing a speech, creating preparation and presentation outlines, delivering a speech extemporaneously, adapting to your audience, and using visual aids. This speech will represent the culmination of the preparation work you have completed, as well as is an opportunity for you to demonstrate skilled extemporaneous delivery.

Audience Analysis for Your Informative Speech

Write an audience survey, a poll, or a questionnaire with three questions that will help you answer the audience analysis portion of the Informative Proposal assignment.

The questions should NOT be opened ended, but should offer the respondent an array of options on a scale that will be easy for you to collate and that will reveal something meaningful about their knowledge of and interest in your topic.

For example:

I know some things about ecoterrorism.

Strongly disagree 1	Slightly disagree 3	Neutral 3	Slightly agree 4	Strongly agree 5

I think ecoterrorism is an important issue.

Strongly disagree 1	Slightly disagree 2	Neutral 3	Slightly agree 4	Strongly agree 5

I am interested in learning more about ecoterrorism.

Strongly disagree 1	Slightly disagree 2	Neutral 3	Slightly agree 4	Strongly agree 5

Alternative format

	not at all		neutral		very much
How much do you personally know about Affordable Care Act (ACA)?	1	2	3	4	5
How much do you care about the ACA?	1	2	3	4	5
How much do you want to learn more about the ACA?	1	2	3	4	5

Another option

Using a scale from 0% (none) to 100% (all), what percentage of students at Marshall University do you believe use Adderall?

Using a scale from 0% (not at all dangerous) to 100% (very dangerous), how dangerous is using Adderall to focus while studying?

Using a scale from 0% (no chance) to 100% (definitely will), what is the chance of suffering negative consequences as a result of using Adderall?

Directions

Use simple statistics to calculate the class average on each of your questions (your instructor will explain how to do this in the class; if you need help, please ask).

Informative Speech Proposal

(50 points)

The electronic template for this assignment is located on the Blackboard. **You must fill in the electronic template and drop it into a drop box for grading and feedback.** The instructors and template are provided here for your convenience and drafting purposes.

FILL IN THE TEMPLATE WITH THE FOLLOWING INFORMATION:

1. Identify the topic of your informative speech. (If your topic is not approved, you will have to submit another informative proposal).
2. Analyze your audience. How is the topic of your speech relevant to your audience? (If it is not directly relevant to the audience, you should select another topic).
3. Write a thesis statement that represents the central idea of your speech.
4. List the main points of your speech (the body).
5. Identify an effective organizational pattern you will use.
6. Provide each of the five oral citations you will incorporate into your speech. You should be able to clearly identify the author of the information provided and his or her credentials. You should use five different sources within the speech. You may not use quotations for the oral citations. **You must paraphrase the information** (put in your own words).

   Examples

   Source: National Institute for Mental Health
   Expertise: Government organization charged with researching and addressing mental health issues in the United States.

   Oral Citation: According to a 2015 factsheet titled "Attention Deficit Hyperactivity Disorder" from the National Institute for Mental Health's website, aspartame and food additives do not cause ADHD. Researchers analyzed existing literature to determine nothing more than anecdotal evidence link these chemicals to ADHD. The Institute cautions parents from relying only on elimination diets to curb symptoms.

7. Provide a full citation sources for the oral citations referenced above in APA or MLA style.

Name: _____   Section: _____   Time: _____

Informative Speech Proposal Rubric

	Points Possible	Points Earned
The topic is appropriate for a brief informative speech. It is narrow and focused.	If your topic is not approved, you will have to submit another informative proposal.	
The audience analysis reports how the topic directly relates to the students in your class.	5	
The thesis statement is appropriate and represents the main point of the speech.	5	
Three main points fit well with the thesis statement.	3	
The Selected Organizational Pattern- is most appropriate for the topic. The pattern will help audience follow and remember the content of the speech.	2	
Five Oral Citations- Five high-quality sources selected, with the topic and audience in mind. Ethos of the speaker or organization being cited is clear (the speaker tells us credentials of the speaker or the organization if we are unfamiliar with the source). Source Named (1) Explanation of Source's Expertise (2) Oral Citation (3)	30	
Five Sources- Complete source citation provided; properly cited in MLA or APA	5	
TOTAL	50	

Informative Speech Proposal Template

NAME:

TOPIC:

AUDIENCE ANALYSIS:

(How is the topic of your speech relevant to your audience? If it is not directly relevant to the audience, you should select another topic).

THESIS:

MAIN POINTS:

    1.
    2.
    3.

ORGANIZATIONAL STYLE:

FIVE ORAL CITATIONS:

1. Source:
Source's Expertise:
Oral Citation:

2. Source:
Source's Expertise:
Oral Citation:

3. Source:
Source's Expertise:
Oral Citation:

4. Source:
Source's Expertise:
Oral Citation:

5. Source:
Source's Expertise:
Oral Citation:

FIVE REFERENCES IN MLA OR APA STYLE

Informative Speech Preparation Outline

The most successful speeches are created with a preparation outline. This outline is a tool you use to organize your ideas and research; it also helps you make sure that your speech is clear and easy to follow. It should be a complete version of your speech in the outline form. The entire speech (introduction, body, and conclusion) should be written in a paragraph format and outlined appropriately. Transitions should be labeled as such and included in a full sentence format. You should include in-text citations and provide references using APA or MLA style.

Rubric for Preparation Outline	Points Possible	Points Earned
Introduction- includes an attention-getting device, thesis, and preview of the main points outlined in a paragraph format. (Each element is worth 2 points).	6	
Main Points- Main points are complete and concise.	3	
Supporting material is from quality sources and supports the thesis well. Information is novel and interesting to a typical audience member.	5	
Five oral citations appear within the text of the speech. The oral citations are complete and a typical audience member can assess the ethos of the source based on the information provided about the source. (Each oral citation is worth 3 points.)	15	
Conclusion- includes a restatement of the thesis, a summary of the speech, and a clincher. (Each element is worth 2 points,)	6	
Transitions are used appropriately throughout the speech. There is a signpost between each main point. Transitions are included within each point as well.	5	
Organization of the speech is clear and appropriate. The main points are presented in a logical format (depending on being logically dependent or logically independent). The information is well organized.	5	
References included follow APA or MLA style (comprised of the five sources cited in the speech and any additional sources consulted to complete the speech).	5	
TOTAL	50	

Name: _____   Section: _____   Time: _____

Informative Speech Writing Formula

Directions: The student can use this as a planning tool for their speech or research papers or it can be used to grade a public speech.

Planning Tools (Speech Objectives)	
1. Topic:	
2. Title:	
3. General Purpose: The general purpose is the broad goal of your speech. Choose one according to the instructions given in class.	_____ to inform _____ to persuade _____ to entertain
4. Specific Purpose: Can start with ➤ To inform my audience about ➤ After listening to my speech the audience will	
5. Central Idea: This is your speech in ONE complete sentence. Your audience should be able to identify the unifying idea/theme/thread that runs throughout your speech.	
I. **Introduction** Your job is to capture the audience's attention; motivate them to listen; establish credibility; and preview what is to come. EVERY step is important!	
A. Attention: Choose one: story, startling statement, quote, question, illustration, humorous anecdote, reference to subject, etc.	
B. Motivation/Benefit: Include ALL three: ➤ Your sources ➤ Your interest in the topic ➤ How the topic will benefit them	
C. Preview: Tell the audience what you plan to talk about. This is your central idea.	
II. **Body** A strong central idea supplies the direction of your ideas. The body is a message that shares a common theme. Develop something that is meaningful and worth listening too. You can change the body to reflect the pattern of organization you are using: chronological, topical, spatial, problem/solution, and so on. Remember the body should have from 2–5 points depending on the pattern of organization you choose.	

From *The Competent Communicator,* Second Edition, by Cristina Doda Cárdenas and Connie Duren. Copyright © 2013 by Kendall/Hunt Publishing Company. Reprinted by permission.

A. Title Your Main Point:
1. Support Material: Use: examples, statistics, testimony, etc.   Include an oral citation if appropriate.
2. Support Material: Use: examples, statistics, testimony, etc. Include an oral citation if appropriate.
Transition/Connective:
B. Title Your Main Point:
1. Support Material: Use: examples, statistics, testimony, etc. Include an oral citation if appropriate.
2. Support Material: Use: examples, statistics, testimony, etc. Include an oral citation if appropriate.
Transition/Connective:
C. Title Your Main Point:
1. Support Material: Use: examples, statistics, testimony, etc. Include an oral citation if appropriate.
2. Support Material: Use: examples, statistics, testimony, etc. Include an oral citation if appropriate.
III. Conclusion
A. Signal the End:
B. Recap/Summary: Reinforce the listener's understanding of the speech by restating the central idea or by simply listing your main ideas.
C. Clincher/Crescendo: End with a quotation, dramatic statements, or reference back to the introduction.
IV. Bibliography (in APA format)

Informative Peer Review Assignment

(20 points)

Students will map the informative speech of an assigned classmate.

This mapping exercise will demonstrate the student's ability to differentiate between a dependent and an independent organization, identify and connect the thesis to the main ideas that support it, and evaluate the information provided. Then, the student will discuss the strongest and the weakest aspects of the content and the delivery, and make at least one or two suggestions for improvement for each area.

On either the template that follows or a worksheet that your instructor provides, you will fill in the following elements for the peer review:

1. Map the speech (include the thesis (2), main points (3), and oral citations (5)). For an electronic submission, you can use drawing tools in Microsoft Word to create the map. (10 points in total)
2. Identify the type of organizational pattern used. Identify whether the main points were logically dependent or independent (your map should reflect this designation). (2 points in total)
3. Was the information provided sufficient, relevant, and compelling? List the oral citations you heard, and discuss how well the oral citations and information provided related to the main points. (5 points in total)
4. Discuss your overall evaluation of the content and delivery of the speech. Briefly discuss the strongest and weakest aspects. Make at least one suggestion for specific improvement(s) for both content and delivery. (3 points in total)

Use the template on the next page to fill in your map.

For an electronic submission, please submit the file as YOURLASTNAME.SPEA KERLASTNAME.INFORMMAP.DOC

Your Name:
Speaker's Name:
Speech Topic:
Date of Speech:

Peer Review Questions

1. Map the speech. Please include the introduction, thesis, main points, and oral citations (10 points).

2. Identify the type of organizational pattern used. Identify whether the speech was logically dependent or independent (your map should reflect this designation; 2 points).

3. Identify the types of evidence and support used in the presentation. Was it sufficient, relevant, and compelling? List the oral citations, and discuss what types of sources these sources represent. Were they evenly distributed throughout the speech? (5 points)

4. Discuss your overall evaluation of the content and delivery of the speech. Make at least one suggestion for specific improvement for content and delivery. (3 points)

Peer Critiquing

Critiquing is the art of evaluating or analyzing a speech. Students should learn to expect feedback about their speeches and accept it with a receptive attitude. Actual practice in the evaluation of speeches can aid you in finding examples, both good and bad, of the criteria which are taught in a public speaking class.

Your Responsibility as a Speech Critiquer

When someone speaks, the assumption, although sometimes faulty, is that someone else is listening. Listening, then, is actually the counterpart of speaking. Certainly in the public speaking process there is no speech without listeners. The listener is one-half of the entire communication process.

In order to fulfill your responsibilities as an audience member in this course, you will be learning and practicing the skill of critical listening. Critical listening means using your abilities and skill to better evaluate the content, organization, language, and delivery of a speaker's presentation.

Since feedback is the primary means by which we learn to improve, especially in the classroom, the specific judgments you make about speech content and delivery need to be presented effectively to the speaker. Commit yourself to becoming the most effective listener you can be. By doing so, you will become a more effective speaker.

Characteristics of Good Critiquing

1. It is objective. If you make a subjective statement, clearly identify it as such. For example, saying "I thought you were dressed professionally" is better than saying "Your dress is pretty."
2. It is definite. Avoid "I'm not sure, but …" Also avoid generalized comments like "Your eye contact was poor," or "You messed up on your visual aid." Say instead, "You often looked at the back wall" or "Your PowerPoint slides didn't have consistent capitalization."
3. It is understandable (organized).
4. It is **constructive** and helpful.
5. It contains praise as well as suggestions for improvement. If you point out a flaw, give a constructive alternative.

Saying "Don't be nervous" is not as helpful as saying "Avoid scratching your nose and straightening your collar."

6.   It avoids ridicule, sarcasm, and intimidation.
7.   It evaluates the **important** aspects of the speech and does not dwell on the minor ones. One "uh" or a passing glance at the back wall is not worth mentioning.
8.   It is the evaluation of a single effort, not a general overall evaluation of past speeches or general speech skills.

Self-Critique: Informative Speech

Length: Approximately 2-3 pages of double-spaced text

Format: 1-inch margins, 12-point font

Write a critique of your presentation based on your recorded speech. Your critique will be graded based on your ability to integrate the class vocabulary into your critique, the use of examples to back up your claims, and the correct use of grammar and spelling.

Objectives

To evaluate one's performance, to reflect on speech preparation, to offer suggestions for improvement on future assignments

Questions to Answer

1. How was the experience of seeing your presentation video? Were there any surprises?

2. How did you feel during the presentation? Were you fully "present" and comfortable? What distracted you (if anything)? What will you do about this for your next presentation?

3. Are you happy with your content choices? If you had to give this speech again, why would you share the same information or choose some other information?

4. Did dimensions of your delivery—eye contact, movement, gestures, and voice—give you the best possible expression of your topic? Explain your answers and provide examples.

5. **Based on the above analysis, name at least three specific things you will work on to improve for your next presentations.**

Each question is worth 3 points.

Grade: /15

Persuasive Speech

For the second major speech of the semester, you will deliver a 6–8 min persuasive speech that addresses a question of policy. You will formulate an argument related to the topic you discussed in your informative speech. For instance, a student who informed the class about physician-assisted suicide might choose to argue for its legalization in West Virginia. A student who raised awareness about child labor involved in making popular products might advocate you to boycott a popular brand known to use child labor. Your speech must contain compelling arguments that use sound reasoning and credible evidence.

This assignment gives you the opportunity to put into practice and demonstrate your ability to prepare and deliver a compelling persuasive speech. To do so, you will work through the speech planning stages you have learned during this course, while taking the unique requirements of a persuasive speech into account.

Persuasive Speech Thesis & Problems Worksheet

What is your topic? (It needs to be a civic issue that addresses the need for a policy change).

What is the argument you want to make? Hint: THIS WILL BECOME YOUR THESIS!
There are two very common structures for a persuasive thesis (use only one):

A.   Actor has failed to perform desired action.
     Example: The West Virginia state legislature must implement affordable college tuition rates.

B.   Undesired action harms us.
     Example: Rising college tuition rates hurt West Virginia students.

Now, with your thesis written, ask yourself WHY? Why is this happening, and why is it bad?
Hint: THESE BECOME YOUR PROBLEMS (You need 3 claims)!
Example: Why has WV failed to implement affordable college tuition rates?
Problem 1: Politicians are not prioritizing higher education.

Why is it bad that we do not have affordable college tuition rates?
Problem 2: Underprivileged students are not attending college.
Problem 3: West Virginians cannot compete in the national workforce.

Formulating a Persuasive Argument

Determining Your Argumentative Focus

When we think about argumentative focus generally, we most often are focused on either the problem or the solution.

Focusing on the Problem

Members of your audience may not consider some issues legitimate problems. For instance, not everyone agrees that climate change is a serious problem. By now, most people accept scientific evidence that climate change is happening. Now, the debate centers on how serious the climate change is and the role man plays in altering the climate. A student who wanted to argue that the U.S. government should enforce strict environmental regulations on carbon emissions may need to "prove" the problem to the audience; that is, climate change is serious and caused by man. Once this has been established through the use of evidence, a straightforward solution can be offered, such as reducing carbon emissions through regulation. You probably do not have time to argue for the legitimacy of your issue and the superiority of your proposed solution.

Focusing on the Solution

Conversely, for other issues everyone agrees that the issue is a problem. For instance, everyone agrees that rape on college campuses is a serious issue. That said, how should we combat the rape epidemic is debated. Different solutions have been offered for this problem. A student speaking about the rape epidemic would not have to persuade the audience that rape is a serious issue. Instead, he would spend most of his or her speech arguing for a specific solution over others (for instance, bystander education mandated at Marshall University).

Think about your topic—do people agree that your issue is a legitimate problem? If not, you will focus on the problem. If people agree that that issue is a real problem, you will likely focus on arguing for a specific solution.

1. What will your argumentative focus be for this speech?

2. What are some "good reasons" people should agree with your argument? Brainstorm reasons why the audience should agree with your thesis.

3. Determine your best reasons. These reasons will help form the foundations of your claims. Shape these reasons into arguments that will help "prove" your thesis.

Persuasive Speech Proposal

(50 points)

The electronic template for this assignment is located on the Blackboard. **You will fill in the electronic template and drop it into a drop box for grading and feedback.** The instructions and template are provided here for your convenience and drafting purposes.

You will type your responses directly into the template provided and **submit via Dropbox.** PLEASE SUBMIT AS LASTNAME.PERSUASIVEPROP.

Instructions

1. Identify the topic of your persuasive speech.
2. Report the results of your audience analysis. What type of audience will you be addressing (see Table 14.2 on p. 301). THE SPEAKER EXPLICITLY EXPLAINS HOW THE TOPIC IS DIRECTLY RELEVANT TO STUDENTS IN THE CLASS.
3. You are asked to present a persuasive speech that is a question of policy. Please explain how you will approach your topic to ensure that you are giving a speech that proposes a course of action or solution to a problem.
4. Write a thesis statement that represents the central argument of your speech. **This statement needs to follow this format: WHO SHOULD DO WHAT?** (Example: The West Virginia state legislature should increase funding for inclusive education in our public schools).
5. What organizational pattern will you use for this speech?
6. List three claims (arguments) you will use to buttress your thesis. These claims help prove your thesis. The claims should be logically related.
7. Provide five oral citations you will use in the speech (you can use oral citations from your informative speech if they reinforce your argument—you will likely need to edit/ tailor them to fit in with the persuasive argument you are making; again, you need five unique sources).
8. Please provide complete citations for each of the oral citations. You may use APA or MLA format.

Persuasive Speech Proposal Rubric

Criteria	Points possible	Points earned
The topic is appropriate for a brief persuasive speech. It is narrow and focused.	Assignment will not be graded without appropriate, pre-approved topic. If topic is not appropriate, you will need to re-do assignment.	
The speaker reports the results of the audience analysis. The student explicitly identifies the type of audience identified in the class (1 point). The speaker also explicitly explains how the topic is directly relevant to students in the class (2 points).	3	
The speaker explains how persuasive argument will be framed as a question of policy.	3	
The thesis statement (the main argument) is an appropriate argument that addresses a question of policy.	5	
Three claims (arguments) that are directly related to the thesis (3 points each). The speaker explains how the claims are logically related (3 points).	12	
Organizational pattern is explicitly stated and the student explains why that organizational pattern was selected for this speech.	2	
Five oral citations (for each oral citation: 1 point for detailing source; 1 point for detailing source's expertise; 2 points for oral citation).	20	
Five references	5	
TOTAL	50	

Persuasive Speech Proposal Template

1. TOPIC:

2. REPORT RESULTS OF YOUR AUDIENCE ANALYSIS. IDENTIFY THE TYPE OF AUDIENCE. ALSO, EXPLICITLY EXPLAIN HOW THE TOPIC IS DIRECTLY RELEVANT TO THE STUDENTS IN THE CLASS:

3. BRIEFLY DISCUSS HOW YOU WILL FRAME YOUR PERSUASIVE SPEECH AS A QUESTION FOR POLICY?

4. THESIS (CENTRAL ARGUMENT):

5. THREE CLAIMS THAT SUPPORT YOUR THESIS. EXPLAIN HOW THE THREE CLAIMS ARE LOGICALLY RELATED:

6. ORGANIZATIONAL PATTERN SELECTED:

7. FIVE ORAL CITATIONS:

   1. Source:
      Source's Expertise:
      Oral Citation:

   2. Source:
      Source's Expertise:
      Oral Citation:

3. Source:
    Source's Expertise:
    Oral Citation:

4. Source:
    Source's Expertise:
    Oral Citation:

5. Source:
    Source's Expertise:
    Oral Citation:

8. FIVE REFERENCES (MLA OR APA)

Rubric for Preparation Outline	Points Possible	Points Earned
Introduction (10 points) includes an attention-getting device (3 points), relevancy statement (1 points), and credibility statement (1 points).	5	
Thesis (6 points) is explicitly stated. The thesis represents the overall argument being advanced in the speech. The thesis should follow the "WHO SHOULD DO WHAT" format.	6	
Claims (9 points) are explicitly presented. The claims directly support the thesis. The claims are arguments that advance the persuasiveness of the speech. There needs to be at least 3 claims in the speech (3 points each).	9	
Evidence/supporting material was from quality sources (10 points) and supported the claims well and was cited correctly (all supporting material needs to be cited in your preparation outline, even if you are not mentioning the source orally in the speech).	10	
Five oral citations (15 points) should be clearly designated within the text of the speech. Three points for each oral citation.	15	
Three persuasive appeals (6 points) should appear in the body of the speech. The speaker should appeal to appropriate emotion, logic, or other psychologically motivating concepts (2 points each).	6	
The body must contain a **refutation** of an appropriate argument from the opposition. The speaker must provide evidence to refute the opposition's argument.	5	
The Conclusion- includes a restatement of the thesis (1 point), a summary of the speech (1 point), and a clincher (3 point each).	5	
The Organization of the speech body was clear and appropriate.	4	
Transitions were used appropriately throughout the speech. (Signpost between each section in the body & transitions within sections).	5	

References Page- At least five references are correctly cited using APA or MLA style.	5	
In full sentence format, accurate spelling, and grammar.	You will just lose points for not formatting (−5) or inaccurate spelling or grammar, or typos (−5)	
TOTAL	75	

Template for Preparation Outline

I. INTRODUCTION
   A. A. Gain the audience's attention in a compelling way:

   B. Thesis (MAIN ARGUMENT—NEED TO BE IN THIS FORM "WHO SHOULD DO WHAT" EXAMPLE: MARSHALL UNIVERSITY SHOULD MANDATE THAT ALL STUDENTS, FACULTY, AND STAFF BE VACCINATED AGAINST THE FLU.):

   C. Relevancy Statement: (WHY IS THIS IMPORTANT TO YOU AND THE AUDIENCE?)

   <**Transition** (to the body of the speech)>

II. **BODY** (NOTE: You may have more sub-main points.)
   A. Main Point 1: STATE THE PROBLEM (EXAMPLE: THE FLU VIRUS IS HIGHLY CONTAGIOUS AND CAN CAUSE SERIOUS CONSEQUENCES FOR THOSE WHO CATCH IT.)

      1. Sub-Point 1: CLAIM (ARGUMENT THAT THE PROBLEM IS SERIOUS—YOU HAVE TO PROVE THAT IT IS SERIOUS TO YOUR AUDIENCE).

         a. Supporting Material: EVIDENCE (SUCH AS ORAL CITATIONS THAT HELP PROVE YOUR CLAIM THAT IT IS A PROBLEM)

         b. Supporting Material: MORE EVIDENCE

         c. Supporting Material: MORE EVIDENCE

      *Make sure within this section you include one persuasive appeal Transition:

2.   Sub-Point 2: CLAIM AS TO WHY THIS ISSUE IS A SERIOUS PROBLEM THAT AUDIENCE SHOULD CARE ABOUT.

   a.   Supporting Material: EVIDENCE THAT PROBLEM IS RELEVANT

   b.   Supporting Material: MORE EVIDENCE

   *Make sure within this section you include one persuasive appeal

<**Transition** (to main point 2)> Now that I have discussed the PROBLEM, I am going to tell you about the best SOLUTION.
B. Main Point 2: STATE YOUR ADVOCATED SOLUTION (LAY OUT THE PLAN).

1.   Sub-Point 1: (YOU NEED TO PROVIDE AN ARGUMENT THAT YOUR PLAN WILL WORK).

   a.   Supporting Material: EVIDENCE FOR THE CLAIM THAT THE PLAN IS GOOD.

   b.   Supporting Material: MORE EVIDENCE FOR YOUR CLAIM

   *Make sure within this section you include one persuasive appeal
   Transition: I have explained my solution, let me tell you about the positive effects it would have if enacted.

2.   Sub-Point 2: POSITIVE EFFECTS OF THE SOLUTION (YOU MAY HAVE MORE/LESS OUTCOMES)

   a.   Supporting Material: Positive Outcome 1

      1.   Evidence for Positive Outcome 1

      2.   Evidence for Positive Outcome 1

Transition: Let me now explain another benefit.

       b. Supporting Material: Positive Outcome 2

          1. Evidence for Positive Outcome 2

          2. Evidence for Positive Outcome

       *Make sure within this section you include one persuasive appeal

3. CLAIM ABOUT WHY THIS SOLUTION IS BETTER THAN ANY OTHER SOLUTION AS A PLACE TO START.

       a. EVIDENCE FOR CLAIM

       b. MORE EVIDENCE FOR CLAIM

4. Sub-Point 4: Refutation (provide a common argument against your position, "Those who disagree with me say . . .."

       a. Supporting Material: Reason # 1 they are wrong

          1. Evidence for Reason 1

          2. Evidence for Reason 1

Transition: I will tell you another reason why critics of my proposed solution are wrong.

       b. Supporting Material: Reason #2 they are wrong

        1. Evidence for Reason 2

        2. Evidence for Reason 2

      *Make sure within this section you include one persuasive appeal

III.   CONCLUSION
     A. Restate the Thesis:

     B. Summary of the main points:

     C. Closing Appeal:

REFERENCES: MAKE SURE YOU INCLUDE REFERENCES WITH YOUR OUTLINE OR YOU WILL LOSE POINTS!

Rubric for Persuasive Speech Presentation

NAME: TIME:		
<u>Introduction</u> includes an attention-getting device, credibility and relevancy statements, and preview of the main points outlined in a paragraph format.	10	
<u>The thesis</u> and <u>Claims</u> are explicit. The thesis represents the overall argument being advanced in the speech. It must be clearly stated in a "Who should do what?" format (10 points). The claims directly support the thesis. The claims are arguments that advance the persuasiveness of the speech. At least three claims are provided. <u>No logical fallacies are used. (15 points)</u>	25	
<u>Evidence/supporting material was from quality sources</u> and supported the claims well. (10 points) <u>Five oral citations</u> should be clearly designated within the text of the speech. The oral citations must include the name of the source and relevant information about the title and date of work being cited. (25 points)	35	
<u>Three persuasive appeals</u> should appear in the body of the speech. The speaker should appeal to appropriate emotion, logic, or other psychologically motivating concepts.	15	
The body must contain a <u>refutation</u> of an appropriate argument from the opposition. The speaker must provide evidence to refute the opposition's argument.	5	
<u>The conclusion</u> includes a restatement of the thesis, a summary of the speech, and a clincher.	5	
<u>Organization</u> of the speech body was clear and appropriate. Problem–Solution or Problem–Cause–Solution patterns are used and appropriate sections are clearly indicated and followed.	5	
<u>Transitions</u> were used appropriately throughout the speech.	5	

Verbal Delivery- **Argumentativeness (5 points)** Rate Vocal variety Articulation, Enunciation, Pronunciation Inflection Use of pauses	20	
Nonverbal Delivery Facial expression Eye contact Physical appearance Movement Gestures	15	
Visual Aid—at least three different visuals presented in Prezi or PowerPoint (no additional words added), or use of an object, model, or demonstration, not to exceed a maximum of six visual aids.	10	
<u>TIME</u> Five (−5) points deducted for every 30 s the speech is under or over the time requirements (6–8 min).		
<u>NOT MORE THAN 10 NOTECARDS USED FOR THE PRE-</u> **<u>SENTATION. FIVE POINTS WILL BE DEDUCTED FOR</u>** **<u>EACH ADDITIONAL NOTECARD.</u>**		
TOTAL	150	

Persuasive Peer Review Assignment

(20 points)

Students will map the informative speech of an assigned classmate.

This mapping exercise will demonstrate the student's ability to differentiate between dependent and independent organization, identify and connect the thesis to the main ideas that support it, and evaluate the arguments and logic provided. Then, the student will discuss the strongest and the weakest aspects of the content and the delivery, and make at least one or two suggestions for improvement for each area.

On either the template that follows or a worksheet that your instructor provides, you will complete the following elements for the peer review:

1. Map the speech (include the thesis (2), main points (3), and oral citations (5)). For an electronic submission, you can use drawing tools in Microsoft Word to create the map. (10 points in total)
2. Identify the type of organizational pattern used. Identify whether the main points were logically dependent or independent (your map should reflect this designation). (2 points total)
3. Was the information provided sufficient, relevant, and compelling? List the oral citations you heard and discuss how well the oral citations and information provided related to the main points. (5 points in total)
4. Discuss your overall evaluation of the content and delivery of the speech. Briefly discuss the strongest and the weakest aspects. Make at least one suggestion for specific improvement(s) for both the content and delivery. (3 points total)

Use the template on the next page to fill in your map.
For an electronic submission, please submit the file as YOURLASTNAME.SPEAKERLASTNAME.PERSMAP.DOC

Your Name:
Speakers Name:
Speech Topic:
Date of Speech:

Peer Review Questions

1. Map the speech. Please include the introduction, thesis, main points, and oral citations (10 points).

2. Identify the type of organizational pattern used. Identify whether the speech was logically dependent or independent (your map should reflect this designation; 2 points).

3. Identify the types of evidence and support used in the presentation. Was it sufficient, relevant, and compelling? List the oral citations and discuss what types of sources these sources represent. Were they evenly distributed throughout the speech? (5 points)

4. Discuss your overall evaluation of the content and delivery of the speech. Make at least one suggestion for specific improvement for the content and delivery (3 points).

Persuasive Speech Reflection

Length: Approximately 2–3 pages of double-spaced text
Format: 1-inch margins, 12-point font

Write a critique of your presentation based on your recorded speech. Your critique will be graded based on your ability to integrate class vocabulary into your critique, the use of examples to back up your claims, and the correct use of grammar and spelling.

Objectives

To evaluate one's performance, to reflect on speech preparation, to offer suggestions for improvement on future assignments.

Questions to Answer

1. How was the experience of seeing your presentation video? Were there any surprises?
2. How did you feel during the presentation? Were you fully "present" and comfortable? What distracted you (if anything)? What will you do about this for your next presentation?
3. Are you happy with your content choices? If you had to give this speech again, why would you share the same information or choose some other information?
4. Did dimensions of your delivery—eye contact, movement, gestures, and voice—give you the best possible expression of your topic? Explain your answers and provide examples.
5. **Based on the above analysis, name at least three specific things you will work on to improve for future presentations.**

Each question is worth 3 points.

Grade: /15

Ceremonial Speech

Professional careers, organizational involvement, leadership roles, and our personal lives often include ceremonies. You will likely be asked to present short speeches for ceremonial occasions. This assignment allows you to practice your ability to connect with an audience through appropriate language and decorum for the situation.

You will prepare and deliver a 3-minute ceremonial speech.

You have many options for the type of speech you present: introduce a speaker, present an award, holiday speech, tribute speech, eulogy, toast, wedding speech, roast, pep talk, or commencement address. You must get the instructor's approval of the topic prior to presentation.

Your goals for this speech include the following: exhibit proper decorum, gain audience's attention, create resonance for the audience, use coherent structure and development, provide substance through supporting material, deliver speech with sincerity and conviction, and give a memorable conclusion.

Planning Your Ceremonial Speech

Topic-

Occasion-

Appropriate <u>Decorum</u>- Please detail how you will address the elements of decorum in your speech:

What level of formality is appropriate for your speech?

How will you build identification with the audience so that your speech resonates with them?

Supporting material- What information will you include in the speech? Will you incorporate any visual aids?

Intensity- What types of emotional appeals will you use? Describe the emotional tone of your voice.

Length (3 minutes)- How will you ensure the speech is 3 minutes?

Example Ceremonial Speech Outline Template

The specific structure of a ceremonial speech will vary depending on the type of speech. I created this template to include the elements that every ceremonial speech could contain. You will want to review the type of ceremonial speech you are giving very closely to make sure that you include the needed elements.

Purpose of Speech:

Theme (what idea and feeling are you trying to convey):

Speech Begins Below:

I.   Introduction
        A. Attention-Getting Statement:

        B. Transition:

        C. Thesis (EXPLICITLY STATE PURPOSE + THEME HERE):

        D. Preview Main Points

II.   Body
        A. Main Point 1 (Connects to Theme):

            1. Example 1 Part 1 (i.e. story):

            2. Example 1 Part 2 (how it relates back to theme):

        Transition:

        B. Main Point 2 (Connects to Theme):

      1. Example 2 Part 1 (i.e. story):

      2. Example 2 Part 2 (how it relates back to theme):

      *Depending on the type of speech, or the length of Main Points 1 & 2, you may have additional Main Points (or not). If you do, just follow the format above.

III.   Conclusion
    A. Restate Thesis:

    B. Summary of Speech:

    C. Conclusion (Toast, Well-Wishes, Appeal to Future- depends on type of speech)

Name: _____   Section: _____   Time: _____

Ceremonial Speech Rubric for Presentation

	Points Possible	Points Earned
Introduction- gains audience's attention. Acknowledges occasion.	3	
Body- supporting material was substantive and creates resonance with audience. The descriptions are vivid. Common values are expressed.	10	
Conclusion- re-acknowledges occasion. Memorable.	3	
Transitions were used appropriately throughout the speech.	2	
Organization of the speech was clear and appropriate.	2	
Verbal Delivery- Rate Pitch Vocal Variety Articulation, Enunciation, Pronunciation Inflection Use of Pauses Use of Emotive Tone (10 points)	20	
Non-verbal Delivery Eye Contact Movement Gestures Visual Aid (5 points)	10	
Total	50	

After-Dinner/Entertainment Speeches

Speech Tips

1. Remember your objective when giving an after-dinner speech is to entertain, amuse or provide enjoyment for your listeners. Emphasis is placed on humor as a vehicle for obtaining audience attention and interest in your views.
2. Humor used in the after-dinner speech is not just comic monologue, it is purposeful. The purpose is to make a point about some facet of society's values or some event of mutual concern to you and your audience.
3. The after-dinner speech seeks to ease the audience into more serious thought rather than beating them over the head with abstract theoretical musings.

Things to Remember When Organizing the After-Dinner Speech

1. Have an effective introduction that captures attention right away.
2. The speech should be more than a listing of stories to amuse listeners.
3. The stories should identify the unifying idea/theme/thread that runs throughout your speech.
4. There should be a gradual leading up to a crescendo in the conclusion that conveys the unifying idea/theme/thread.

A Sequence to Follow When Writing an After-Dinner Speech

1. Relate a story or anecdote, present an illustration, or quote an appropriate passage.
2. State your unifying idea/theme/thread that is implied by your opening remarks.
3. Follow with a series of additional stories, anecdotes, quips, or illustrations that support or prove your unifying idea/theme/thread. Use supporting material to develop each story in a coherent manner.
4. End with a restatement of the unifying idea/theme/thread you have developed. As in step 1, you can use another quotation or a final story that provides a sense of closure.

Name: _____   Section: _____   Time: _____

Grading Rubric for PowerPoint

Instructions: You are to provide a PowerPoint presentation with each speech you present. Include a printed version with your grade form, audience analysis, and typed outline. It is your responsibility to read the chapters on how to design and use this medium. Below are ten guidelines you will be graded on and should observe when developing and using your Power-Point. You should have a cover slide, introduction, one slide per main point, conclusion slide, and source citation slide at a minimum.

_____ 1. Cover page contains:
  ◆ Name of student
  ◆ Name of college
  ◆ Name of speech
  ◆ Course name/section

_____ 2. Uses an effective design template
  ◆ Use as few words as possible to present your idea
  ◆ Use concise titles
  ◆ Maintain design consistency
  ◆ Apply the same style and typeface for titles throughout
  ◆ Uses a typeface that is large enough to be seen and is easy to read
  ◆ Avoid busy backgrounds that make the information hard to read

_____ 3. Uses color appropriately
  ◆ Color can stimulate the senses
  ◆ Color can help the audience to see comparisons, contrasts, and emphases
  ◆ Be aware of the cultural association to color

_____ 4. Slides are simple (uncluttered)

_____ 5. Uses graphics and animation wisely

_____ 6. Avoids wordy text slides: **no more than eight words to a line and eight lines to a slide**

_____ 7. No misspelled words

_____ 8. Visual adds clarity and interest to the speech
  ◆ Should have at least three pictures or images in the presentation
  ◆ Should enhance the message and exist for a visual sake

_____ 9. Source citation page (located after the conclusion)
  ◆ Is included in the PowerPoint
  ◆ Utilizes APA or MLA format

_____ 10. Effective use during delivery
  ◆ Student faces the audience, not the slides
  ◆ Student does not read from the slides or the computer screen

From *The Competent Communicator,* Second Edition, by Cristina Doda Cárdenas and Connie Duren. Copyright © 2013 by Kendall/Hunt Publishing Company. Reprinted by permission.

Stealing or Just Borrowing? An Inference and Fact Exercise

Directions: Answer the following questions. Based on the story below, are the following statements, True, False or not known. Mark the appropriate answer. The question mark represents the not known answer choice.

> A homeowner had just turned off the lights in their living room when a woman appeared and demanded something of value. The owner opened the wall safe. The contents of the wall safe were taken and the woman left. The police were called immediately. When the police arrived they noticed the window was open.

True   False   ?

❏ ❏ ❏   1. A woman appeared after the homeowner had turned off the lights.

❏ ❏ ❏   2. The thief was a woman.

❏ ❏ ❏   3. The thief did not demand money.

❏ ❏ ❏   4. The person who opened the wall safe was the home owner.

❏ ❏ ❏   5. The homeowner took what was in the wall safe and left the house.

❏ ❏ ❏   6. A person opened the wall safe.

❏ ❏ ❏   7. The woman and the homeowner live in the house together as a married couple.

❏ ❏ ❏   8. Do we know how much money was in the wall safe?

❏ ❏ ❏   9. The thief demanded money from the homeowner?

❏ ❏ ❏   10. The story mentions only three persons: the homeowner, the woman who demanded something of value and the police.

From *The Competent Communicator,* Second Edition, by Cristina Doda Cárdenas and Connie Duren. Copyright © 2013 by Kendall/Hunt Publishing Company. Reprinted by permission.

Basic PowerPoint Requirements

All students need to follow these guidelines when creating their slideshows:

Number of Slides

- Don't use your PowerPoint as your speech note cards.
- For a five to seven minute speech you should avoid an excessive amount of slides (i.e., 10+). Hit key points.

Blank/Title Slides

- Use a blank slide or a title slide at the beginning of your slideshow.
- If you use a title slide, it can have the title of your presentation on it but usually does not include your name, the date, and your class time.
- Insert a blank slide at the end of your slideshow. It should be the same background color that you have used throughout the slideshow.
- Utilize a blank screen whenever there is a time lapse between the information to be presented from one slide to the next.

Color

- Don't overuse. Be consistent with the same background color for each screen.
- When using a template (wallpaper background), make sure it is appropriate for the speech topic.
- Choose one color for titles and a separate color for text (unless instructed otherwise by your instructor).
- Maintain consistency in color of fonts.
- Choose a color for letters that contrasts with the slide's background (dark-colored letters on pale/light backgrounds and light-colored letters on dark backgrounds).

Fonts and Spacing

- Maintain consistency in choice of font (make sure it is not a font that is difficult to read/see).
- Size of font needs to be large enough for entire audience in the back of the room to see (minimum of 44–point for titles and 32–point for text).
- Boldface fonts if they are not already bold.
- Follow the "6–7 words/6–7 lines" rule to avoid a screen that is too busy or crowded.
- Maintain consistency in capitalization for titles and text.
- Use upper and lower case lettering (not all caps) for all titles and text.
- Maintain consistency in spacing.
- Frame/border your pictures/art when appropriate.

From *Experiences in Public Speaking,* Sixth Edition, by Marla D. Chisholm and Jackie Ganschow. Copyright © 2015 by Kendall Hunt Publishing Company. Reprinted by permission.

- Avoid too much blank space on slides.
- Align bullet points. Do not center them.
- Maintain even margins.
- Do not overlap letters and pictures. Words become difficult to read.

Wording

- Use phrases (not full sentences) for your text.
- Use parallel structure.
- Use correct grammar and spelling. Utilize the grammar and spelling checker.

Visual Images

- Use images related/appropriate to speech content.
- Use clip art, pictures, charts, etc. that are clear (not fuzzy) and large enough to be seen in the back of the classroom.
- Don't overuse visual images; avoid too many images on one slide. One good picture or drawing is usually sufficient. Two images/pictures are the limit on a single slide.
- Leave a margin around the edge of slides.
- Do not put text too close to pictures/images.
- Do not use cartoons or images that have a watermark stamp on them.
- Crop copyright information from pictures and images.

Animation and Sound

- Avoid distracting animation.
- Do not use sound unless you have incorporated streaming video.
- Adjust volume for streaming video so it is loud and clear.

Transitions and Custom Animation

- Use appropriate/non-distracting transitions and maintain consistency between every slide.
- Use "custom animation" when appropriate and be consistent in the form chosen (bring in one piece of bulleted information/full phrase at a time).

Matching Analogies

Directions: Match the first half of the analogies to the second. Then decided whether the analogy is literal or figurative. Finally, analyze the completed analogies to decide whether they adequately analyze the subject or are far-fetched.

1. Saying ADHD exists is like . . . _____
   (Literal or Figurative)
2. Cutting arts funding in schools would . . . _____
   (Literal or Figurative)
3. Not teaching the Trail of Tears is like . . . _____
   (Literal or Figurative)
4. Building a wall on the U.S. borders is like . . . _____
   (Literal or Figurative)
5. Assisted suicide is just as humane as . . . _____
   (Literal or Figurative)
6. Bailing out auto companies is like . . . _____
   (Literal or Figurative)
7. Removing books from school libraries is like . . . _____
   (Literal or Figurative)
8. Not drug testing athletes is like . . . _____
   (Literal or Figurative)
9. Refusing HPV vaccine is like . . . _____
   (Literal or Figurative)
10. Photoshopping people in magazines is like . . . _____
    (Literal or Figurative)

Options

- . . . euthanizing an animal.
- . . . taking candy from a baby.
- . . . not watching students during an exam.
- . . . building a mote around a castle.
- . . . refusing to vaccinate children.
- . . . affect students the same as cutting math.
- . . . saying Santa Clause is not real.
- . . . removing the Holocaust from history curriculum.
- . . . putting make-up on a pig.
- . . . handing out Get Out of Jail Free Cards.

Incorporating Language Devices Into Your Speech

You are asked to think about how you can use language strategically in your persuasive speech and create language devices to incorporate into your speech.

I would like you to first think about how to use the following devices in your speech. Please provide a specific example for each of the following types of language devices and how you could use it in your speech.

1. Simile or Metaphor:

2. Parallelism:

3. Alliteration:

4. Antithesis:

5. Invitation to Imagine:

Integrating Presentation Media

Please brainstorm a plan for your presentation medium below. Provide a brief explanation about why you chose this type of a presentation medium. Be ready to answer the following questions. How would this presentation medium:

1. Draw the attention of the audience to your topic?
2. Illustrate an idea that cannot be fully described by words alone, clarify a key point, and/or help your audience deepen their understanding?
3. What would be the advantages and disadvantages of using this type of medium?

Finally, create a draft of what you plan to use as a presentation medium below.

Planning Your Notecards

Your speech delivery should be extemporaneous. The two best ways to ensure extemporaneous delivery are to use note cards for delivering the speech and to practice your speech multiple times. You should plot out what would be exhibited on your note cards. You should use a max of ten notecards for presentations in our class.

Here is a suggested formatting of notecards:

> CARD 1- Introduction—contains an Attention-Getter keyword, Thesis in Bold, and a keyword of the main point preview
> CARD 2- Main Point 1, Sub-point 1, Oral Citation(s) for Sub-point 1, and any other keywords needed to cue material. Word "transition" appears at the bottom to remind you to transition
> CARD 3- Sub-point 2, Oral Citation(s) for Sub-point 1 and any other keywords needed to cue material. Words "SIGNPOST TRANSITION MP1 TO MP 2" appear at the bottom to remind you to transition.
> CARD 4- Main Point 2, Sub-point 1, Oral Citation(s) for Sub-point 1 and any other keywords needed to cue material. Word "transition" appears at the bottom.
> CARD 5- Sub-point 2, Oral Citation(s) for Sub-point 1 and any other keywords needed to cue material. Words "SIGNPOST TRANSITION MP2 TO MP 3" appear at the bottom to remind you to transition.
> CARD 6- Main Point 3, Sub-point 1, Oral Citation(s) for Sub-point 1 and any other keywords needed to cue material. Word "transition" appears at the bottom.
> CARD 7- Sub-point 2, Oral Citation(s) for Sub-point 1 and any other keywords needed to cue material.
> CARD 8- Conclusion- Thesis, Summary of the Main Points, Clincher

You should use keywords as much as possible and make the cards readable when they are held at stomach-level. They are meant to cue you, not ever to be read to the audience. Put whatever sourcing info you need for the oral citations to be accurate, but not so much that you are tempted to read it.

Again, I want to remind you that less is more. You should begin practicing with your outline and then move to practicing with your notecards. Although I do not want you to memorize your entire speech, you should memorize your thesis, main points, and the sourcing elements of your oral citations.

CPSIA information can be obtained
at www.ICGtesting.com
Printed in the USA
LVHW02s0320010618
579219LV00003B/12/P